# PUTTING LEARNING FIRST:

## Governing and Managing the Schools for High Achievement

**A Statement
by the Research
and Policy
Committee
of the Committee
for Economic
Development**

**CED**

**Library of Congress Cataloging-in-Publication Data**

Committee for Economic Development.          Research and Policy Committee.
    Putting learning first   :   governing and managing the schools for high achievement.
    p.  cm.
    "A statement by the Research and Policy Committee of the Committee
for Economic Development."
    Includes bibliographical references.
    ISBN 0-87186-100-3 : $17.50
    1. School management and organization — United States.  2. School supervision —
United States.  3. Academic achievement — United States.  4. Education and state —
United States.     I. Title.
LB2805.C62  1994
371.2'00973 — dc20                                        94-22399
                                                          CIP


First printing in bound-book form: 1994
Paperback: $17.50
Printed in the United States of America
Design: Rowe & Ballantine

COMMITTEE FOR ECONOMIC DEVELOPMENT
477 Madison Avenue, New York, N.Y. 10022
(212) 688-2063

2000 L Street, N.W., Suite 700, Washington, D.C. 20036
(202) 296-5860

# CONTENTS

# PUTTING LEARNING FIRST:

**Governing
and Managing
the Schools
for High
Achievement**

# RESPONSIBILITY FOR CED STATEMENTS ON NATIONAL POLICY

The Committee for Economic Development is an independent research and policy organization of some 250 business leaders and educators. CED is nonprofit, nonpartisan, and nonpolitical. Its purpose is to propose policies that bring about steady economic growth at high employment and reasonably stable prices, increased productivity and living standards, greater and more equal opportunity for every citizen, and improved quality of life for all.

All CED policy recommendations must have the approval of trustees on the Research and Policy Committee. This Committee is directed under the bylaws which emphasize that "all research is to be thoroughly objective in character, and the approach in each instance is to be from the standpoint of the general welfare and not from that of any special political or economic group." The Committee is aided by a Research Advisory Board of leading social scientists and by a small permanent professional staff.

The Research and Policy Committee does not attempt to pass judgment on any pending specific legislative proposals; its purpose is to urge careful consideration of the objectives set forth in this statement and of the best means of accomplishing those objectives.

Each statement is preceded by extensive discussions, meetings, and exchange of memoranda. The research is undertaken by a subcommittee, assisted by advisors chosen for their competence in the field under study.

The full Research and Policy Committee participates in the drafting of recommendations. Likewise, the trustees on the drafting subcommittee vote to approve or disapprove a policy statement, and they share with the Research and Policy Committee the privilege of submitting individual comments for publication.

*Except for the members of the Research and Policy Committee and the responsible subcommittee, the recommendations presented herein are not necessarily endorsed by other trustees or by the advisors, contributors, staff members, or others associated with CED.*

# CED RESEARCH AND POLICY COMMITTEE

---

*Voted to approve the policy statement but submitted memoranda of comment, reservation, or dissent. See page 55.

viii

# PURPOSE OF THIS STATEMENT

Frustration has become the watchword of education reform. For well over a decade, policy makers, business leaders, and many educators have been calling for a major overhaul of our nation's stagnating system of public education. Yet, in terms of improved student achievement, we have precious little to show for all the rhetoric, goal setting, and haphazard experimentation. Why has the progress of school restructuring been so glacially slow?

To CED's trustees, who, since the early 1980s, have devoted a large portion of their time, energy, and resources to developing practical solutions to the nation's educational malaise, the answer is clear. When it comes to public education, our nation has lost its sense of priorities. Instead of focusing on what is most essential—improving learning and achievement—our society has turned the schools into social, ideological, and financial battlegrounds. Those who govern and manage our schools—the educational decision makers—heap mandate upon mandate on our frontline educators but provide very few effective incentives and tools to encourage teachers to teach or students to learn. Instead of rewarding accomplishment, those in charge of education reward procedural compliance and discourage substantive innovation.

*Putting Learning First: Governing and Managing the Schools for High Achievement* reorders our nation's educational priorities. It recognizes that we have been burdening the schools with too many different and unproductive missions, and as a result, very few are being done well.

*Putting Learning First* builds on a solid foundation of policy research and analysis conducted by CED's trustees over more than a decade. CED's landmark 1985 policy report *Investing in Our Children: Business and the Public Schools* emphasized that high standards and a rich curriculum are necessary components of excellence in education and that the most important work of learning takes place in the interaction between teacher and student. Three subsequent CED education reports were *Children in Need: Investment Strategies for the Educationally Disadvantaged* (1987), *The Unfinished Agenda: A New Vision for Child Development and Education* (1991), and *Why Child Care Matters: Preparing Young Children for a More Productive America* (1993). These reports focused the attention of policy makers, business leaders, and the public on the critical importance of children's early development for later school success and on the need to provide school-age children with the social and health supports that will help them learn in the classroom.

## A NEW WAY OF WORKING

*Putting Learning First* calls for major behavioral changes that must be made by those who govern and manage the schools. It articulates an effective incentive structure for students, teachers, and administrators; it proposes new ways of organizing the schools to support learning and achievement; and it places central responsibility on communities and states for providing the health and social services that children need to support their ability to learn, thereby freeing schools to focus on their primary mission of academic achievement.

The report focuses on governance and management and does not try to address other learning issues, such as curriculum content and methods of instruction. We believe that such matters are best left to teachers and principals, in consultation with parents and the community. We also chose in this report not to address the potential of new computer and telecommunications technologies for increasing the productivity and effectiveness of learning. CED recently began a project on "Improving Mathematics and Science Education and the Use of Technology in the Classroom" to develop recommendations for improved utilization of new learning technologies by teachers and students.

## ACKNOWLEDGMENTS

On behalf of CED's Research and Policy Committee, I would like to express our deepest appreciation to Roy J. Bostock, chairman and chief executive officer of D'Arcy, Masius, Benton & Bowles, Inc., for the energy, purposefulness, and insight he brought to his chairmanship of the CED subcommittee that developed *Putting Learning First*. Our gratitude also goes to the exceptional group of business leaders and educators, listed on pages viii and ix, whose dedication, intellect, and experience contributed to the dynamic subcommittee sessions that led to the report's powerful policy recommendations.

Special thanks are due to the CED staff members who provided the solid research and analysis on which the recommendations are based and whose writing skills are reflected in a very readable document: Project Director Sandra Kessler Hamburg, CED vice president and director of education studies; Project Editor Claudia P. Feurey, CED vice president for communications and corporate affairs; Van Doorn Ooms, CED senior vice president and director of research; and Terra Geiger, CED policy analyst. Finally, I would like to acknowledge the important financial and intellectual contributions made by the many private and corporate foundations, listed on page 57, that have so generously supported this CED project.


Josh S. Weston
*Chairman*
*Research and Policy Committee*

# Chapter 1
# INTRODUCTION AND SUMMARY

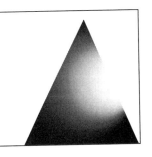

Is America serious about educational excellence in its public schools? A hard look at the evidence suggests it is not. After more than ten years of "reform," American students are performing no better than in 1970. In international comparisons, they do relatively well in reading but routinely turn in poor showings in mathematics and science, and the gap does not appear to be narrowing. According to the National Assessment of Educational Progress, only 7 percent of U.S. seventeen-year-olds can handle complex math problems involving algebra, and only 20 percent can write at an adequate level.

Those who set education policy *do* seem serious about *calling* for educational excellence. But in the same breath, they add mission upon mission, mandate upon mandate, onto already overburdened schools, diluting and deflecting the schools' ability to fulfill their educational goals. Furthermore, they tend to define those goals more in terms of what goes into education, such as teacher/pupil ratios, per-pupil expenditures, or compliance with regulatory requirements, than what is supposed to come out—learning and achievement.

CED believes that there can be no significant progress in education reform—and no lasting improvement in educational achievement —until those who govern the system change the way schools are organized and managed. Accordingly, this policy statement offers a comprehensive strategy for improving the governance and management of the nation's public school system.

The recommendations we make grow out of four strongly held, interrelated beliefs:

- **Public schools are fundamental to a strong American society.** A failing public education system is more than a threat to our economic future. It is a threat to our very existence as a free, democratic people.

- **The primary mission of the public schools should be learning and achievement.** Schools should solidly ground all students in language and mathematical skills and provide them with a broad base of knowledge in subjects such as literature, science, foreign languages, history, social sciences, and the arts. Students should be able to use and apply this knowledge. Academic course work for all students should be rigorous and substantial.

- Schools play an important role in socializing youngsters and preparing future citizens, and they should continue to do so. Schools should teach, by word and example, the values of self-discipline, teamwork, fair play, truthfulness, personal integrity, and respect for others. **But, schools are not social service institutions;** they should not be asked to solve all our nation's social ills and cultural conflicts. States and communities must lift the burden of addressing children's health and social needs from the backs of educators. They must, of course, arrange needed services for children and their families, often in collaboration with the schools. But other state and community agencies should pay for and provide these services so that schools can concentrate on their primary mission: learning and academic achievement.

- **The current emphasis on compliance with regulations should be reduced.** Instead, there should be greater reliance on creating effective incentives for principals, teachers, and students to raise academic achievement. Both successful and unsuccessful performance must have consequences. School systems should reward teachers and administrators for improving the performance of their students, not merely for seniority and credentials. Students must come to believe—with reason—that their achievement in school will have important implications for their adult lives.[1]

## WHY GOVERNANCE AND MANAGEMENT MATTER

The real *work* of learning happens in the classroom, in the interaction between teacher and student. This interaction is affected by innumerable large and small decisions made by principals, school boards, superintendents, state legislatures, education department officials, and the federal government. These decisions and their implementation can either aid or hinder quality education in the classroom. This is the heart of education governance and management.

*Governance* is the process by which people and institutions set the policies that guide our schools, provide incentives for implementing those policies, and supply the resources that enable the schools to operate. *Management* is the process by which district administrators, principals, and teachers put those policies into practice and use those resources in their schools. The policies created by governance, through their influence on management decisions and teacher and student behavior, have a profound effect on what happens in the classroom.

CED believes that our education governance system, as currently operating, is a serious barrier to improving our schools. Yet, governance has been one of the most neglected areas of education reform. Few major reform initiatives of the past ten years have attempted to define the roles and responsibilities of different levels of governance or to improve the abilities of the individuals and institutions responsible for making critical educational decisions.

We know that schools *can* improve achievement. Schools that have high academic standards *and are organized to achieve them* are successful. Yet, we also know that many schools are not organized effectively to support learning. This is due in part to poor management at the school and district levels, but it is also the product of a governance system that is ambivalent about the schools' mission and that rewards compliance with mandates rather than improvements in student learning.

There are, of course, many superintendents, principals, teachers, and parents who work hard to sustain and improve their schools. But school administrators, teachers, and students respond to incentives created by policy makers. Unless we reestablish learning as our fundamental educational goal and provide those in the schools with both the incentives and the operational flexibility to reach those goals, we are unlikely ever to see more than scattered islands of true educational quality.

## A NEW WAY OF THINKING

Although the state governments have the ultimate authority over education, the local school board is the primary institution of American education governance. Public confidence in school boards is at an all-time low. The United States has nearly 16,000 separate school districts, and boards of education nationwide are awash in bitterness and contention as they wrestle with divisive political and social agendas. Instead of giving clear academic direction, most school boards are micromanaging their schools' day-to-day operations. Many of America's public school systems are facing governance gridlock. They are preoccupied with, and sometimes paralyzed by, nonacademic issues. Many recent reform proposals, such as charter schools, school choice, and voucher initiatives, have tried to solve educational problems by bypassing local boards. This loss of confidence in school boards is also reflected in the steady expansion of state control over education throughout the last decade.

We strongly support local governance of schools but stress that there must be a major overhaul of the role and operations of local school boards. Local institutions are best able to formulate policy to meet the different needs of different communities. This does not imply that we support "business as usual" at the local level. On the contrary, local school boards must stop micromanaging individual schools and become true *educational policy boards*, with the responsibility to set achievement goals, provide resources and incentives to achieve those goals, and ensure accountability.

In order to become effective policy-making bodies, school boards must establish and articulate a clear and commanding vision of educational success for their communities and craft a coherent educational agenda that reflects this vision. Boards must promote policies and practices that support this agenda and must defend them from those with narrow agendas who would constrict or inhibit what teachers may teach and limit what students may learn.

Similarly, state governments should establish an educational vision, ensure that local educational authorities are able to fulfill that vision, and hold local districts accountable for their performance. They should normally not be running individual schools and should refrain from issuing mandates that interfere with legitimate local objectives and the day-to-day operation of schools. State education bureaucracies that seem to exist only to enforce state and federal mandates should instead provide local districts with technical support. They also should be pared down where possible as a matter of efficiency and reduced regulatory responsibility.

These changes would allow decision making on curriculum and day-to-day management issues to rest primarily in the school. Those closest to where education takes place —the principal, teachers, parents, and students

—would have the authority they need to make their schools true communities for learning.

The federal government must also change its way of doing its educational business. Although the federal government provides only about 6 percent of all public school funding, these resources and the rules that accompany them have a profound effect on state and local practices. Historically, federal policy and funding have focused on assistance to the disadvantaged, the disabled, and other students with special needs and, to a lesser degree, on educational research. Federal policy in all categorical programs should emphasize incentives and greater flexibility for schools so that they may reach achievement goals.

In recent years, the federal government has also assumed a new and increasingly powerful role as a leader and a catalyst for educational improvement. The passage of the Goals 2000: Educate America Act, which was signed into law in 1994 with strong bipartisan support, gives the federal government a valuable new platform from which to provide leadership in support of academic excellence. Goals 2000 creates a framework for establishing and implementing high and clear national standards for what students should know and be able to do, assessments based on those standards, and inducements to achieve them.

Through new incentives and seed money, Goals 2000 can motivate state and local officials, teachers, parents, and administrators to concentrate on academic achievement. By itself, the act cannot win the war against educational apathy and neglect, but it is a serious call to arms.

## SETTING ACADEMIC STANDARDS

**The first priority of those who govern education should be to establish learning and achievement as the primary missions of the schools.** Currently, communities, states, and the national government are asking those who manage our classrooms to be parent, social worker, doctor, psychologist, police officer, and perhaps, if there is time, teacher. Clearly, schools have a critical social-development role to play in students' lives. But we believe that those who govern our schools must *put learning first*. They have major responsibilities for academic standards and achievement. They should set rigorous content and performance standards that clearly indicate what students should know and be able to do. And they must develop and implement tools to evaluate performance.

This policy shift will help those at the school level to develop rigorous academic curricula, indicate areas where schools need to improve, and send the message to students that society expects high academic achievement. **We enthusiastically support rigorous and substantive national standards and assessments in a wide range of subjects as an integral component of efforts to raise student achievement**.

We urge states to use these national standards to develop clear content and performance goals but not to create rigid curricula mandating exactly how schools should achieve them. We also urge states to limit their goals to *measurable* academic achievements and to avoid adopting vague, values-laden, "life-style" goals and objectives.

This is not to say that those who govern the schools do not have a responsibility to set standards of behavior for students and school personnel. CED has consistently stressed the importance of the "invisible curriculum" as integral to the schools' educational mission.[2] The messages that schools send about what is expected, what behavior will and will not be tolerated, and how students and adults should treat each other can enhance or destroy classroom learning.

## REWARD ACHIEVEMENT, NOT COMPLIANCE

High academic standards will mean nothing without accompanying changes in the behavior of superintendents, principals, teachers and other school personnel, and students. Policy makers have two primary alternatives for influencing behavior in the school system:

mandating changes in the rules by which schools operate or creating incentives — financial, professional, or social — that reward improved student performance. Governing by mandate, currently the norm, rewards compliance, emphasizes procedure, and discourages innovations that breach the rules. In contrast, a system of incentives, which stresses positive motivation and allows flexibility and experimentation, is more likely to produce achievement for different types of students with different needs. CED believes that policies that reward school personnel and students for raising academic achievement offer the most promise for improving our education system.

## RELIEVING SCHOOLS OF THE SOCIAL AGENDA

The social changes this country has undergone in recent decades, especially the problems of poor and disadvantaged children and families, have sent our public schools reeling. Schools that were designed to educate a generally stable student population from generally stable families are now challenged by families in turmoil, violence, drugs, poverty, ill health, and destitution of both purse and spirit.

By both decision and default, much of the burden of dealing with these massive national problems has been placed on the public schools. Many look to the school instead of to parents and community as the frontline defense against every social or health problem from teen pregnancy to child abuse, AIDS, violence, and religious disaffection.

No organization can traverse such a swamp of conflicting missions. Yet, most schools in urban areas and many in suburban and rural communities are pursuing, willingly or not, ever-expanding social and ideological agendas. Few schools have the money, trained personnel, time, or capacity to respond to the increasingly complex social-support needs of their students.

And what is the result of these growing social mandates? School after school is accomplishing neither its academic nor its social goals.

New social agendas can swiftly overtake schools. For example, for reasons more ideological than educational, some schools are placing medically fragile and emotionally disturbed students in the care of teachers who have no training or background in dealing with their needs and are providing those teachers little or no additional help and resources. New pressures to remove nearly all disabled students from special education classes and place them in regular classrooms are overwhelming many schools, which must comply to avoid lawsuits or reductions in funding. Too many students have been wrongfully or carelessly classified as learning disabled over the years, with devastating effects on these students' lives. But now many schools are mainstreaming *all* disabled students with little regard for the nature or severity of the students' disabilities, their ability to function in a regular classroom, the educational benefits they derive, or the impact on other students.

There is, of course, a significant difference between assuming primary responsibility for a social service agenda and carrying out legitimate educational functions to ensure that students are ready and able to learn. Effective education has always been closely connected with targeted efforts to address conditions that limit students' readiness to learn, and schools have traditionally responded to the social and economic needs of their communities. Although the challenges that confront the schools have changed, students' reliance on schools and social service agencies to meet a broad range of needs has not. We urge continued strategic innovation drawing on successful models to enhance collaboration between schools and social service agencies.

Communities have some responsibility to prepare their children for school, to equip them to take advantage of education, and to help meet their social and health needs as they grow toward adulthood. Schools are often the only "checkpoint" for identifying children's health and social problems. And in many communities, school buildings are the most logical institution in which to locate services. But the schools are only *one institution*, and their first mission is to educate.

Community problems need to be addressed through community-driven services and institutions. CED has been a strong advocate of early intervention for improved school readiness and of access to needed health and social services for youngsters of school age.[3] These services may be *placed* in the schools, they may be *delivered* through schools, but they should not be made the *responsibility* of the schools.

States and communities have numerous social service institutions that can and should provide students and families with the social and health support they need. State and local education leaders should coordinate their activities with those of their counterparts in the political and social service arenas to make this happen, possibly under an existing or new umbrella authority. Although funding and service delivery should come from outside, when services are located in the school building, the school principal should oversee them, and the superintendent should coordinate them in the district.

## THE RESPONSIBILITIES OF GOVERNANCE

The actual form that governance takes, such as whether school boards are appointed or elected, is less important than whether policy makers clearly understand their responsibilities and have the capacity and the incentives to carry them out. The following are the essential tasks for those who govern education. They are obligations, not guidelines, and none can be ignored. Those in charge of overseeing our schools should:

- First, and above all, state clearly to the community that learning is the fundamental goal of schools.

- Ensure that all policies support learning and achievement and that they are well coordinated and coherent.

5

- Set goals for achievement, based on state and national standards, to guide the performance of students and school personnel and monitor student achievement to measure progress in attaining these academic goals.

- Ensure that resources are adequate to meet stated goals.

- Delegate responsibility and authority, including the authority to innovate within appropriate guidelines, and hold those with such authority accountable for making progress toward achievement goals.

- Design and implement incentives that reward teachers, students, and administrators for improving learning and establish more effective methods for dealing with teachers and administrators who perform poorly.

- Maintain vigorous communication with parents and the community to stress the importance of learning and to involve families and others in the learning enterprise.

- Coordinate policies and activities with related government and private institutions that are responsible for child development, health, welfare, and other services.

- Support, gather, and disseminate research and information that help schools develop educational programs to fit their students' needs and give parents a means to evaluate their schools.

## PUTTING LEARNING FIRST

The landscape of public education is thick with agendas competing for attention, and schools nationwide are saddled with burdensome and inappropriate political, social, and ideological missions. When society feels it cannot cope, it turns to the schools.

Our first message for those who set policy for our schools and run them on a daily basis is: Clear away the extraneous and the second-ary. No institution can be everything to everyone, and no institution can succeed if it has too many competing goals. The primary mission of the public schools is to provide the children in their care with substantial knowledge and sound academic skills.

Our second message is that we *can* improve our schools. America's children *can* reach the achievement levels our society desires and needs. The vast majority of the people who govern, manage, and teach in our schools are committed professionals and dedicated civic volunteers who want the schools to succeed. There are strong leaders in our schools, and that leadership needs to be encouraged. If those who govern, manage, and work in our schools succeed in concentrating the mission of the public schools on learning and achievement, we believe that all American students will be better served and better prepared for the next century.

But this will require major changes in our systems of governance and management, changes that will come up against many entrenched interests. All sectors of the community, including business and the media, are needed to support the public schools visibly and vocally by making learning and achievement primary community values.

Do we have the political will to achieve the goals set forth in this statement? The answer is far from clear. Far too many Americans appear to be content with our 1970s skill levels, in spite of the fact that our work force will soon have to meet twenty-first century competition. A study of employer, parent, and student views on educational quality developed for CED found a striking disparity between parents and students, who tend to be satisfied with their schools, and employers, who feel that a large majority of their new hires lack adequate writing and problem-solving skills.[4]

Moreover, American students spend far less time in school and far less time on academic subjects than students in Japan, France, and Germany, with high school students in these nations receiving more than twice as much core academic instruction as American students.[5]

Our country cannot be content with mediocre academic performance. Such mediocrity hinders our economic performance and will erode our democratic and social institutions. Wherever the political will does not already exist to make systemwide educational changes such as those outlined in this statement, business and civic leaders, government officials, and educational officials who understand the importance of those changes must work to engender it.

We believe that it is in our collective power to choose excellence over mediocrity. But to do so, we must demand it, expect it, reward it, and support it in every student, parent, teacher, administrator, and local, state, and federal education official.

And we must begin today.*

*See memorandum by ARNOLD R. WEBER (page 55).

# Chapter 2
# SCHOOLS THAT EDUCATE

The mission of the nation's public schools has always been to ensure that children acquire the knowledge and skills necessary to function productively as citizens and workers. This mission has not changed, but its requirements have. For most of this century, it meant providing most students with only basic skills and knowledge; relatively few were expected to master rigorous academic content, complete secondary school, or continue on to higher education.

This approach is no longer sufficient. Many analysts attribute the decline in the wages of our low-skilled workers to increased use of technology and higher skill requirements in the workplace. If the United States is to raise living standards for all its citizens, Americans must be able to work with substantially greater knowledge and skills. Unfortunately, after more than a decade of education reform involving countless experiments, substantial funding increases, and endless rhetoric, educational achievement still lags behind what the nation requires.

## THE U.S. ACHIEVEMENT GAP

In the past, much of the contribution of elementary education to economic growth has come from increases in the "quantity" of education. Although there is still room for improvement (about 15 percent of twenty-four- to twenty-five-year-olds do not have a high school diploma), much of the future contribution will have to come from increasing the "quality" of students graduating from our high schools.[1]

Yet, results from the National Assessment of Educational Progress show that in most subjects, average American students perform at about the same level as they did in the early 1970s. Among seventeen-years-olds, although a slight gain in reading has been measured in the past twenty years, no significant changes in writing or math skills have been found. Science scores are significantly lower than in 1970.[2]

Although most students appear to master low-level skills, few show capacity for complex reasoning and problem solving. For example, in 1990, fewer than 10 percent of seventeen-year-olds could "infer relationships and draw conclusions using detailed scientific knowledge" or "synthesize and learn from specialized reading materials."[3] These more advanced skills, which ask students to apply what they learn in different situations, are becoming more important in a job market where flexibility, innovation, and adaptability are essential.

Recent and past international assessments repeatedly show that in math and science, American students do not compare well with their counterparts in other countries.[4] Although U.S. average reading performance tends to rank high internationally, not all U.S. students are well schooled in reading.[5] While this may reflect the great economic and cultural diversity in our population, we can no longer afford to use diversity as an excuse not to raise the performance of all students to high achievement levels.

Americans are increasingly skeptical of "school reform," especially when it requires more of their tax dollars. Citizens are losing faith in the ability of schools to educate anyone, especially students with social and cultural impediments to learning.

Such impediments are real and widespread. Our culture increasingly promotes instant gratification over hard work, discipline, and deferred benefit. The average student spends twelve times as much time watching television as reading for pleasure.[6] Others work long hours at after-school jobs, leaving them little time for schoolwork and reinforcing a peer culture in which learning and achievement are less valued than immediate purchasing power. Recent research confirms this cultural dilemma: The achievement of immigrant children appears to decline as they become more "Americanized."[7]

## SCHOOLS *CAN* EDUCATE

Against this backdrop, can schools really make a difference in student achievement, especially for the disadvantaged? We believe they can. In spite of the prevailing skepticism, research has shown that schools that value high academic standards and are organized to achieve them are successful, even after allowing for differences in student backgrounds.[8] These successful schools share several common characteristics:[9]

- A clear mission focused on academic learning

- High standards for achievement and a rich course content

- Teachers and principals who have control over the organization of their school and authority over school resources

- A principal who is both a skillful manager and a strong instructional leader

- Students who feel they are part of a community in which the adults reinforce positive values about learning and work*

- Parents who support the school's mission, participate in school programs, and support their children's learning in the home

In short, these schools are true "communities for learning," in which faculty, students, and parents shape a common educational vision and make learning and achievement their top priorities.

Although successful schools are more common in affluent communities, such schools can and do exist in less affluent and disadvantaged areas. A study contrasting inner-city Catholic schools, public magnet schools, and public comprehensive high schools in New York City and Washington, D.C., found that the inner-city Catholic schools generally succeed because they have a focused mission, high standards, and committed parents. Public schools that shared these characteristics also succeed.[10] These more successful public schools in urban areas are generally magnet or special-purpose schools, sometimes called *focus schools* (see page 10).[11]

## THE KEYS TO REFORM: LEADERSHIP AND RESPONSIBILITY

School boards and state education departments often look for simple solutions to what, in reality, are complex problems. They may look at a list of "what makes schools effective" and, in a mechanical fashion, order schools to adopt those characteristics. For example, a school board may see that every successful school has an identifiable mission and order its schools to create one. The school principal appoints a committee of teachers who write a mission statement, which is then placed on school bulletin boards and sent home to parents.

That is usually as far as it goes. Teachers, administrators, and students continue to follow their daily routines; and little, if anything, changes. Such mandates only establish compliance with rules and regulations as the central goal for school personnel; they do not inspire better performance. Most successful businesses know that management by compliance and control is not an effective way to run an organization. Organizations that set goals but give flexibility to local units and provide rewards for solving problems are more likely to have employees who aim for and produce desired results.[12]

Similarly, successful schools start with high standards for academic performance and then

---

*See memorandum by PRES KABACOFF (page 55).

## CHARACTERISTICS OF FOCUS VERSUS GENERAL-PURPOSE SCHOOLS

| Focus Schools | General-Purpose Schools |
| --- | --- |
| They have clear, uncomplicated missions centered on outcomes and the ways they intend to influence the performance, attitudes, and behavior of their students. | They have diffuse missions defined by the demands of external funders and regulators; they focus on delivering programs and following procedures rather than on outcomes. |
| They are strong organizations with a capacity to initiate action in pursuit of their missions, to sustain themselves over time, to solve their own problems, and to manage their external relationships. | They have little capacity to initiate their own solutions to problems, define their internal character, or manage their external relationships. |
| Students and staff consider them to be special. | Because they reflect a standard model established by central authorities, staff and students have less reason to feel any ownership of the school. |
| They have strong social contracts that communicate the reciprocal responsibilities of administration, students, and teachers and establish the benefits that each derives from fulfilling the contract faithfully. | They allow staff and students to define their own roles in the school. |
| They aggressively mold student attitudes and values, emphasizing secular ethics of honesty, reliability, fairness, and respect for others. | They see themselves primarily as transmitters of information and imparters of skills. |
| They have centripetal curricula that draw all students toward learning certain core skills and perspectives. | They sort students according to ability and offer profoundly different curricula to different groups. |
| They are problem-solving institutions, taking initiative to change their programs in response to emerging needs. | Their ability to solve problems is constrained by external mandates and rigid internal divisions of labor. |
| They protect and sustain their distinctive character, both by attracting staff members who accept the schools' premises and by socializing new staff members. | They have little capacity to select staff or influence the attitudes or behavior of new staff members. |
| They consider themselves accountable to the people who depend on their performance — parents, students, neighborhood and parish groups, and financial supporters. | They answer primarily to bureaucratic superiors — outside rule-making, auditing, and assessment organizations. |

SOURCE: Paul T. Hill and Tamar Gendler, *High Schools of Character* (Santa Monica, Calif.: The RAND Corporation, 1991).

adjust their educational programs to the needs of the student body. When the faculty, usually with the involvement of parents, make decisions on the things that matter most for learning—curriculum, instruction, and school climate—student achievement is likely to improve.[13] This need for flexibility makes it unlikely that the United States can mandate its way to education excellence.

## DECENTRALIZING MANAGEMENT FOR MORE EFFECTIVE SCHOOLS

Although a few school systems are beginning to practice more participatory management, most still labor under the outmoded *compliance-and-control* model of governance and management. **We believe that compliance and control must be replaced by more flexible management that gives more authority and accountability for results to teachers, administrators, parents, and students. This "flatter" management structure must be coupled with a variety of incentives, focused on measurable academic achievement, that will motivate improved performance.**

Decentralizing schools through various forms of *site-based management (SBM)* has been one of the most popular reform strategies of the past decade. Unfortunately, most initiatives that call themselves site-based management do not in fact transfer management to the school. A RAND Corporation analysis of pioneering experiments with SBM in five large school districts (Columbus, Ohio; Dade County, Florida; Edmonton, Alberta; Jefferson County, Kentucky; and Prince William County, Virginia) found that most experiments were short-circuited by poor design and excessive interference from school boards and state authorities.[14] Often, mixed messages were sent and unrealistic expectations held. In several of the school districts studied, including Columbus, Ohio, the school board and superintendent encouraged SBM while mandating changes in curriculum, instruction, textbooks, and teacher responsibilities. In Los Angeles and Montgomery County, Maryland, the boards threatened to cancel their SBM experiments if unmistakable gains in teacher satisfaction or student achievement did not occur within one or two years.[15]

Chicago is another example of conflicting messages and expectations. In 1988, the Chicago schools were reorganized to give the community real authority over individual schools. During the first attempts at reform, the central administration was reluctant to give real power to the schools, even though it was called for in state law.

Although Chicago's site-based management has shown some progress, improvements in student achievement have yet to be demonstrated. A 1993 study by the Consortium on Chicago School Research of the University of Chicago found that about 40 percent of the city's elementary schools are making "systemic educational improvements" that are likely to boost student achievement. About a third of elementary schools have created "strong democracies" in which the principal, teachers, parents, and community leaders collaborate effectively on school improvement.

From 1989 to 1991, the Chicago schools' central administration staff was reduced by about 12 percent. Future plans include a fundamental reexamination of the role of the central office.[16]

Although site-based management has not been shown to improve academic performance, we believe this is due more to a failure to adopt genuine SBM and to couple it with incentives for student achievement than to flaws in the concept. Most SBM experiments have focused on relationships among the adults in the school and between the school and the central office; very few have defined student achievement as a central goal, and very few studies of SBM have used improved achievement as a criterion for success.[17] Teachers and principals have little incentive to implement strategies to improve academic performance if achievement is neither established as a goal nor used as a basis for evaluating their effectiveness.

## LINKING SHARED DECISION MAKING TO STUDENT ACHIEVEMENT

There are many successful schools that employ the flexibility of site-based management to raise student achievement, although these efforts are generally not identified as SBM programs. For example, schools in the "Success for All" network link teachers, principals, and parents in a collaborative effort to redesign their schools' instructional practices to emphasize high-level skills for all students. "Success for All," developed by Robert Slavin and his associates at The Johns Hopkins University, intensively develops reading, writing, and language skills from kindergarten to third grade. The program currently operates in eighty-five schools in nineteen states.

When learning problems appear, "Success for All" provides intervention that is immediate, intensive, and minimally disruptive to the students' regular program. With the assistance of tutors, reading classes are reduced from twenty-five students to fifteen, all of whom require the same level of instruction. Assessments, done every eight weeks, identify students who need tutoring or other types of assistance, such as family intervention.

In each "Success for All" school, at least 80 percent of the teachers must agree to implement the program. The experience of many of the schools in the network has shown that the program can be implemented without any significant increase in funding, but the board and administration must allow the school to use Title I, special education, and other state compensatory education funds to emphasize prevention and early intervention rather than remediation. "Success for All" has also been shown to save money by significantly reducing grade retentions and placements of students in special education.

"Success for All" also provides early intervention for health or family problems that may be holding a child back academically. Each school is expected to configure social workers or counselors into a family-support team that can connect families with appropriate community service agencies, provide parenting education, and involve parents in their children's success in school.

An extensive evaluation of the program shows that students in "Success for All" schools are performing significantly better than students in control groups at all grade levels from one to three and that the longer a school is in the program, the greater the improvement. Effects are particularly significant for students in the bottom 25 percent of their classes.[18]

The Accelerated Schools network, created by Henry Levin of Stanford University, represents another successful model in which site-based decision making drives school organization, curriculum, and instructional strategies (see page 13).[19]

**What Decentralized Management Requires of School Boards and Other Stakeholders.** Moving decision making down to the school level requires consistent, compatible support from above. Unless those who govern the schools provide school personnel with clear direction on standards and curriculum, as well as consistent technical support, school-site management is unlikely to result in improved student achievement.[20] Accordingly, school boards and superintendents should set goals and monitor their schools' progress as they work toward those goals while encouraging risk taking and innovation by those at the school level.[21]

Widespread adoption of site-based management will transform, but not diminish, the crucial leadership role of the school superintendent. The superintendent should continue to set the tone of the district and ensure that board policies are reflected in school-based activities. Because the superintendent will remain primarily accountable for the success or failure of the school system, he or she must be well versed in the best educational practices and able to transmit this thinking in a way that inspires responsible innovation by the schools.

Good relationships between schools and other community institutions and agencies, such as child care providers and preschools, libraries, museums, community centers, health clinics and hospitals, and a variety of social service and family-support organizations, are essential. Although a school's principal should oversee the operation of any services that are located in the school building itself, each of these services is governed by its own agency, funding, and rules. It is unlikely that a principal would have the capacity to organize an array of services for his or her school without help from others in the community. A governance structure that represents the entire community can facilitate policy and resource decisions that allow these institutions to function cooperatively and interdependently.

We do not advocate delegating all management functions to individual schools. Some functions, such as purchasing and warehousing, transportation and food service, negotiations with unions, research and development, and technical support services, could benefit from economies of scale and may be better managed districtwide. Each school board and superintendent should determine the most effective way to divide management responsibilities between schools and the central administration.

A RAND study of decentralization and accountability identified specific actions that the school board and central administration

---

## ACCELERATED SCHOOLS

The aim of the Accelerated Schools Program, developed by Stanford University Professor Henry Levin, is to restructure a school so that at-risk students are brought into the educational mainstream. Dr. Levin believes that traditional remediation slows down student progress, resulting in children already at risk who fall further and further behind the rest of the students. He argues that at-risk students need an enriched, high-quality, and high-content school experience that will help them learn at a faster rate. A number of studies have found that when at-risk children are exposed to high-content instruction designed to create understanding, they not only learn basic skills but also are more successful at developing advanced skills.

The full transformation to an Accelerated School takes about six years. Facilitators selected by the school district and the individual school go through rigorous training at Stanford University or one of the Satellite Centers. There they acquire the management tools that will enable them to work effectively with teachers and administrators at the school site. The first two pilot schools were launched in 1987; by fall 1992, some 300 elementary and middle schools in twenty-five states had begun the process of transformation.

Each Accelerated School is expected to develop a unity of purpose, initiate school-site decision making and responsibility for results, and create an instructional approach that builds on the strengths of students, teachers and administrators, other staff, and parents.

School-site decision making shared among educators, parents, and the community is a crucial feature of an Accelerated School and encompasses curriculum, instructional strategies and materials, personnel, and allocation of resources. The district is expected to provide needed support services in the areas of information, technical assistance, staff development, and evaluation, as well as an appropriate system of student and school assessment for accountability purposes. The process provides particularly strong professional incentives for teachers and other staff by linking their efforts to attainable goals.

Accelerated schools have documented increased attendance of both students and teachers, substantial increases in parental participation, higher achievement scores, and waiting lists for enrollments.*

*Henry M. Levin, "The Necessary and Sufficient Conditions for Achieving Educational Equity" (paper prepared for the Commissioner's Education Equity Study Group of the Department of Education in New York State, November 1992).

must take to make site-based management work:[22]

- The school board must make site-based management the central tenet of restructuring, not just one of many different and conflicting reforms.

- School authorities must support school personnel as they experiment and take risks and not shift direction at the first sign of difficulty.

- School boards and superintendents must give up their direct control over schools and increase the capacity of central administration to provide technical and material assistance to school personnel.

- The central office must help schools coordinate their programs so that students are prepared for promotion from one school to the next.

- The board and administration must provide school personnel, who are not used to taking responsibility for curriculum or resource allocation, with training and quality information with which to make decisions. The administration must build planning time into the school day so that site-based management is seen as integral to the work of teachers and principals and so that it is not perceived as yet another overly burdensome addition to their regular duties.

Despite the lack of direct evidence on site-based management's impact on achievement, we believe that moving decision making to the school site will help raise school performance. However, SBM is only a means to better achievement; it is not an end in itself. As such, it must be coupled with clear achievement standards, incentives, and lines of accountability that are aimed at improved academic performance of students.

**We recommend making site-based management a central part of a new system of school-based accountability in which the school's faculty, in consultation with parents and others in the school community** and within a framework of rigorous academic standards, is given real authority to make decisions on curriculum, instruction, personnel, and the use of school resources. In exchange, school personnel must meet achievement goals set forth in a long-range education investment plan or performance contract. These contracts should articulate the school's mission, specify goals for student achievement, and describe how the school will use its resources to meet those goals.

Los Angeles has incorporated these principles into its ambitious school restructuring agenda, known as LEARN (Los Angeles Educational Alliance for Restructuring Now). This program, which will eventually be implemented throughout the Los Angeles Unified School District, is designed to fundamentally alter decision making and accountability for achievement (see page 15).

**Training Is Essential.** In the private sector, business devotes about 1.4 percent of payroll to training, and many high-performance organizations devote considerably more. Schools, on the other hand, expend as little as 0.5 percent of budget on staff development, and this is typically among the first areas to be cut when resources are lean.[23] Lack of sufficient training in decision making is one of the reasons site-based management often does not work. It is wrong to ask schools to accept responsibility for management without technical know-how. Training for teachers and principals should be an integral part of any plan to decentralize management to the school level. As much as possible, this training should be designed to meet the needs of individual schools.

**The Role of School Principal.** Under the collaborative SBM model that we advocate in this statement, the principal's leadership is critical. To lead a school effectively, the principal must be both an expert manager of resources and an inspiring educator who sets the tone and direction of the school. The principal must be able to foster collaboration among the faculty and ensure that the concerns and ideas of parents and students are heard. Working with teachers and parents, the principal must set standards of achievement and discipline for the students and mediate any disputes that may arise. Sharing power is essential. A principal who demands to be the sole voice of authority is simply duplicating the command-and-control mentality of traditional school bureaucracies.

The principal must also have the authority to oversee any noninstructional social and health services that are located in the school to ensure that the professionals who deliver those services are acting in a manner consistent with the school's mission and standards of behavior. Finally, the principal must act as an ambassador for the school to the larger community so that collaborations with business and other public- and private-sector institutions can be developed and sustained.

Good leaders are more often made than born; leadership skills can be learned and nurtured through training and experience. Teachers traditionally become principals by taking a program of administrative courses at a graduate school of education that generally

---

## LOS ANGELES EDUCATIONAL ALLIANCE FOR RESTRUCTURING NOW

LEARN is a comprehensive education reform and restructuring agenda for the Los Angeles schools that was developed by a broad-based coalition of leaders from Los Angeles's diverse education, ethnic, business, labor, academic, religious, and social advocacy communities. Work on the LEARN framework, titled *For All Our Children*, was begun in 1991; in March 1993, the board of education unanimously adopted the plan for phased-in implementation throughout the 630-school district. The first 34 schools were recruited in June 1993; and in June 1994, 60 schools were added.

LEARN is promoting fundamental changes in school governance and management. It moves decision making and budget authority to the school level (the schools will receive eighty-five cents of every budget dollar). Under the plan, the role of the school board and the central administration will be to set policy and performance standards and provide oversight to ensure that schools are meeting their goals. LEARN schools will offer college-oriented curricula as well as vocational training options for every student. LEARN provides numerous opportunities for parent participation and will invest heavily in training for teachers and principals to expand their grasp of effective management techniques and cutting-edge instructional strategies. Training and development are being conducted

through a partnership among three key organizations: UCLA's School Management Program, the Los Angeles Educational Partnership (LAEP), and the Los Angeles Unified School District (LAUSD). An evaluation mechanism is being developed. The key components of this partnership are:

- UCLA's Advanced Management Program for principals and lead teachers at each school site

- LAEP's Learning Community Program, which is building the capacity for change within the larger school community to promote teamwork

- LAUSD's Professional and Stakeholder Development Program, which provides an extensive array of technical support services to bolster the reform effort at each school

- UCLA's New Directions Program, which provides leadership training for school board members, collective-bargaining specialists, and senior and midlevel district and regional administrators

Since its inception, LEARN has been supported by an extensive array of corporate and foundation donors. In the future, LEARN will operate within the limits of available school funding, with most of the school- and district-level changes supported through the reallocation of existing LAUSD resources.

teach little about fostering collaborative relationships. Few districts provide prospective principals with opportunities to develop the kind of leadership skills that are required for decentralized, collaborative management. A higher priority should be placed on identifying and developing principals who are strong instructional leaders and effective administrators and who are able to flourish in a collaborative environment.

One of the most interesting programs to nurture talented principals is the National Principals' Leadership Academy at the University of Delaware (see below).

## THE ROLE OF UNIONS IN SCHOOL REFORM

No significant or widespread improvement in schools is possible unless unions are constructive participants in the process. About 85 percent of teachers, the central participants in school reform, belong to unions. Contracts negotiated by unions and management commonly specify teacher responsibilities, pay scales, and other issues that affect school organization. Whether by state law or simply habit, labor-management relations in most districts continue to be confined to a narrow scope of bargaining for wages, benefits, and working conditions, as if collective bargaining did not have important consequences for school operations and student achievement.[24]

We believe that both school officials and union representatives want to build quality schools. However, the adversarial industrial union model, which emphasizes the divergent, rather than common, interests of teachers and district officials, remains all too prevalent. Although such a model may be consistent with a centralized compliance-and-control mode of governance and management, it is not compatible with a system that promotes teacher authority and responsibility. Collaboration is essential; neither unions nor district officials can create quality schools alone. Unions cannot empower teachers to reorganize schools without working through school districts, and district officials cannot reorganize schools or alter the duties and responsibilities of teachers without working with the elected representatives of teachers.[25]

In practice, district-union collaboration will require compromises based on mutual trust and the desire for positive change. District

---

## NATIONAL PRINCIPALS' LEADERSHIP ACADEMY

This program at the University of Delaware helps effective principals build on their success by bringing together resources from both education and business. The program is sponsored by the U.S. Department of Education and the University of Delaware and has received the endorsement of fifteen state governors.

Each year, thirty principals are selected on the basis of their success in carrying out school-based change and their ability to contribute to the academy. Principals are nominated by someone in their school, the central administration, or the school board.

The program is built around a professional concept of the school principal: Principals should be committed to research-based ideas about good learning, they should be able to recognize quality teaching and know how to nurture it, and they should understand what gets in the way of good teaching and how to eliminate those obstacles. The program is based on the notion that true leaders have a vision for their school and a strategy for effecting change. The program strives to develop leaders who are team players, who can facilitate collaborative decision making, and who can work successfully with their superintendent, central office, school board, and the community.

The program includes a two-week intensive course in July, opportunities to communicate with program faculty and other participants during the year, and a five-day review in March.

administrators must allow unions and teachers a strong voice in designing reform strategies, including professional and curriculum concerns as well as traditional collective-bargaining items. In return, unions must allow more collective-bargaining flexibility on such items as the allocation of teachers within districts, pay schedules, and teachers' roles and responsibilities. Both district officials and unions must rally their own constituents around school-system restructuring and discipline those who fail to support the enterprise.

Union-management collaboration on school restructuring will not eliminate the need for collective bargaining; teachers' and administrators' unions will always have interests that diverge from those of school boards and central office management, and these differences must be negotiated. But both unions and management need to see that their best interests will be served by working together toward the goal of greater student achievement. It is the duty of the school board, the school administration, and the union leadership to align their goals for the district and to forge a real culture of responsible cooperation.

## CHARTER SCHOOLS: TESTING DECENTRALIZED MANAGEMENT AND DEREGULATION

A growing number of states are authorizing the creation of public schools that operate autonomously, free from local district and state regulations, in exchange for an agreement to improve student achievement. These autonomous schools, known as *charter schools,* have been in existence only since 1991. Now eight states have collectively granted about 100 charters, and charter legislation is pending in twelve additional states.[26]

Unlike regular public schools, charter schools are organized by individuals or groups, rather than school boards. The charter contracts with a sponsor, usually a designated government body such as the state or a local school board. The contract is binding; the sponsor can revoke or refuse a charter if a school does not meet its goals. Charter schools are usually funded on a per-pupil basis by the state at the average amount spent per pupil in the state.

Charter schools have the potential to advance school reforms in several ways. Like regular public school choice programs, charters can challenge other public schools in the area to improve their academic programs. Also, charter schools offer an opportunity to experiment with decentralization without lengthy delays and impediments. Finally, state-chartered schools can serve as a tool to induce change in recalcitrant local school boards.

Most current charter school initiatives will have limited effects. Most states limit the number of charters allowed in the state or in an individual district. Also, in many cases, the charter must be issued by the local school board, which may be reluctant to give up control of the resources that follow a child to a charter school. Finally, in some states, teachers face salary uncertainty and job insecurity by moving to charter schools, seriously weakening their incentive to leave regular public schools. On the other hand, charters offer an opportunity for increased autonomy and innovation in the public school system.

**In spite of the limitations of current initiatives, CED enthusiastically supports experimentation with charter schools. We believe charter schools offer an opportunity to complement regular public schools and to demonstrate the ability of site-managed schools to meet student achievement goals in a less restrictive regulatory environment. However, state authorities should require charter schools to meet basic civil rights and health and safety statutes, and charters should be held accountable for high achievement standards through the same types of assessments that we recommend for other public schools.**

## SCHOOL CHOICE: USING PARENTAL PREFERENCES TO IMPROVE PERFORMANCE

Of all the governance reforms that have been proposed for improving school performance, the most controversial is *school choice,* which allows parents and students to choose among schools, with public resources following the student. Public school choice plans may provide for selections within a school district or between districts. Private school choice allows students to use public resources at nonpublic schools.

Choice introduces an element of competition into the educational system. In principle, the threat of losing students and resources should motivate schools to make changes that would better satisfy students and their families. Choice advocates assume that these changes would also improve educational quality.

**Public School Choice.\* We believe that allowing parents to choose the public school their child attends can provide a valuable incentive for schools to improve performance**. The necessity of improving performance can encourage each school to define its mission, curriculum, and teaching strategies more clearly. Choice can also invigorate school faculty, especially if they are given more latitude to be creative, and if teachers are allowed to move more readily from school to school to find a teaching environment that best suits their skills and interests. If public school choice provides an opportunity for students to enter programs that most effectively meet their needs, it should improve children's learning and achievement.

Choice offers an *incentive* to improve, but it is not a *substitute* for the hard work of improvement itself; it therefore must be accompanied by other changes. For instance, schools must have effective control over the learning process if they are to compete for students, and this implies easing federal and state regulatory constraints in favor of more school control over the use of resources, including personnel.

Similarly, choice, in principle, should improve equity by providing more attractive school alternatives to lower-income families that cannot afford to find better schools by moving, a strategy widely employed by the more affluent. In practice, these gains may be very limited for families that have little knowledge of or access to quality schools. There is evidence that better-educated and more affluent parents are more likely to take advantage of choice.[27] However, where efforts have been made to provide parents with good information and some assistance with transportation, these problems have been mitigated. For example, for the school year 1989-90, 3,600 out of the approximately 10,000 children participating in Minnesota's Second Chance choice program reported their families had received welfare benefits during the past five years. Statewide during the same period, only about 21 percent of students were eligible for free or reduced lunches, indicating that low-income youngsters were more than significantly represented in the choice program. Similar findings were reported for children from non-English-speaking homes.[28]

We support the following criteria, developed for the Minnesota statewide choice plan by Joseph Nathan of the Hubert Humphrey Institute of the University of Minnesota, as useful design guidelines:[29]

- There should be a list of academic and other performance goals that all schools must include in their programs.

- The plan should assist parents in selecting among various programs for their children.

- Entrance requirements should promote racial integration and must not discriminate on the basis of past achievement or behavior.

- All schools within a given geographic area must be given encouragement and assistance to develop distinctive features, rather than allowing resources to be concentrated in a few magnet schools in that district.

---

\*See memorandum by JAMES Q. RIORDAN (page 56).

- There must be opportunities for teachers and principals to help create distinctive, quality programs.

- Transportation must be provided within a reasonable area for all students.

- The program must include continuing oversight and modification.

We are also concerned that the transfer of resources from poorer to more affluent districts under interdistrict choice plans may widen resource disparities between districts if many students choose to transfer. This underscores a dilemma: Schools have less incentive to improve if there are no penalties for failure. Nevertheless, we urge that school choice plans be designed to ensure that adequate resources remain available for schools in which significant efforts for improvement are under way. This could be accomplished, for instance, by financing arrangements that rewarded such efforts independent of student enrollments and transfers.

**Vouchers.** Our enthusiasm for well-designed public school choice plans does not extend to the use of tax-supported vouchers for private education. Although we recognize the merits of having independent private schools and respect the choices of those who can afford and prefer them, we have grave reservations about using scarce *public* resources, which would otherwise be available to improve *public* education, to support them. Choice and competition are useful, but we believe they can be employed most productively for our society within the public system.

Public education is our society's basic instrument for conveying democratic principles to children, for incorporating new immigrants into American society, and for promoting racial, ethnic, and cultural integration. We fear that private school choice would foster social fragmentation and weaken our democratic institutions.

All the difficulties that might attend public school choice, such as limited information and access, would apply to vouchers to at least the same degree. There are other problems as well. We have seen no voucher proposal that would require private schools to compete with public schools on an equal basis. For example, California's 1993 voucher initiative would have exempted both existing private schools and any public schools that chose to accept vouchers from educational standards and would have allowed them to discriminate on the basis of academic ability, religious belief, family income, and English-language proficiency (see page 20).[30] Even Catholic schools in inner-city neighborhoods, which have a record of successfully educating poor children, are able to exclude students who are low achievers, have discipline problems, or have special needs. If the nation expects public schools to be held accountable for student achievement, it is unreasonable to give tax dollars to schools that are not required to meet the same standards. We believe that all schools receiving public money should be held accountable, using appropriate assessments of student performance, whether they are governed publicly or privately.

Although there is considerable political and ideological support for private school vouchers, there have been no wide-scale applications on which to base conclusions about the impact of vouchers on student achievement or educational opportunity. The current experiment in Milwaukee, which allows a very small percentage of poor children to attend private schools at public expense, is too limited to provide any general lessons. After three years, the results are mixed, with no substantial improvements in student achievement, although other benefits, such as greater parental satisfaction, have been found.[31] Because of the small number of children allowed to participate, the schools they are leaving have few incentives to improve.

A more extensive voucher initiative was begun in Puerto Rico at the beginning of the 1993-94 school year. The Puerto Rican government is providing eligible children from second grade through high school with a voucher for $1,500 that can be used at any public or private school. To be eligible, a family must have income of less than $18,000 a year. Because annual per capita income is only $6,500 in Puerto Rico, a majority of public school children are eligible for a voucher. Since the average cost of private school tuition in Puerto Rico is under $1,700, the $1,500 voucher is a considerable sum. Although the part of the voucher program that transfers public funds to private schools was recently ruled in violation of the Puerto Rican constitution by a superior court judge, the ruling is being appealed, and the program, as of July 1994, was still in effect.

The program is too new to evaluate. Of the 1,809 students participating in the first year (out of a student population of 450,000), over 1,181 have moved from one public school to another, 311 have left public school for private school, and 317 have transferred from a private to a public school. One of the most interesting aspects of the plan is that the voucher offers a student moving into any public school a supplement to the resources the commonwealth already provides for each pupil, making low-income pupils an attractive catch. The budget for the program is currently $10 million, and there are plans to expand it to $30 million in 1997. Puerto Rico has implemented other governance and management reforms

## CALIFORNIA VOUCHER PROPOSAL

In November 1993, California voters were given the option of approving a state constitutional amendment that would have fundamentally altered the governance and financing of the state's education system. Proposition 174 would have provided vouchers to parents of school-age children that could be used at any public, private, or parochial voucher-redeeming school. The amount of the voucher was set for at least half of the state's current per-pupil expenditure or $2,600. Under the amendment, all public schools would have been allowed to convert to "scholarship-receiving schools." As such, they would be held only to the standards that currently govern private schools, which consist of minimal health and safety regulations, reporting of student attendance, and criminal record checks of faculty. Other than that, there were no specified performance standards or fiduciary responsibilities.

Unlike the private schools, public schools would continue to be held accountable for student achievement, fiscal competency, and meeting myriad state and federal educational and social mandates. Unlike the public schools, which may not turn away any students, private schools would have the right to expel any student who would not "derive substantial aca-

demic benefit" and would not be required to accept any child who had a handicapping condition or who did not speak English. Because the amount of the California voucher was set at $2,600 per child with no flexibility for children who need more costly special education, private schools would have had little incentive to accept such students unless the parents were able to supplement the tuition. The California voucher plan would also have initially cost the state treasury at least $1.3 billion to subsidize tuition for current private school students, whose parents tend to have higher incomes than parents whose children attend public school. It was estimated that nearly one-quarter of public school students would have to transfer to private schools before the program would break even financially.

Voters in California rejected Proposition 174 by more than 2 to 1, and there was strong opposition from the business community. Even the governor, who initially supported the voucher idea, opposed it in the end because of its potential damage to the state treasury. Supporters of the voucher initiative are planning to redraft the proposition to take some of the criticisms into account and put it on the ballot in November 1994 or 1995.

SOURCE: Children Now, *What School Choice Means for Children* (Oakland, Calif.: Children Now, September 1993).

as well, including a phased-in school-site management program that will involve all schools by 1998.[32]

If frustration with the public schools continues to grow, it is likely that the number of voucher proposals will increase. Those who govern the public schools must take them seriously. However, the experience with vouchers has been too limited to judge their effects on either the achievement of students or the social and political goals of public schooling. **Therefore, we do not at this time find the arguments supporting vouchers persuasive enough to reverse our long-standing objection to using public funds to support private education.**

**We recommend that government officials and school governance authorities monitor the results of existing state and local voucher initiatives carefully and impartially to determine their potential effects on student achievement, social diversity, and other important goals of the educational enterprise. Future voucher proposals should be evaluated against three key criteria:**

- **Private schools accepting vouchers should be held accountable for student outcomes in the same ways we are now proposing for public schools.**

- **Participating private schools should not be allowed to discriminate on the basis of race, ethnicity, religion, or a student's past academic performance.**

- **Public schools in the area should be given the latitude and the support they need to innovate and compete effectively with private schools.**

## PERFORMANCE INCENTIVES: MOTIVATING HIGHER ACHIEVEMENT

Providing incentives to enhance performance is basic to good management. Incentives spell out the rewards for good performance and the consequences of failure. In successful businesses, the goals employees are expected to attain are generally well defined, as are the key indicators of success: output, quality, and bottom-line financial performance. Appropriate rewards or consequences, such as pay, promotion, and demotion, are linked to these goals and indicators. Public schools, however, rarely follow such practices.[33]

Teachers and administrators are seldom rewarded for improving student learning. More often, they are rewarded for correctly following procedures, such as handing in attendance registers on time or following a lesson plan.[34] Not only is improved student achievement not rewarded, but in most public schools there are few consequences for teachers or principals if students fail. In fact, in many schools, teachers and principals are punished for showing initiative that does not comply strictly with the rules.

For students, too, the system's preoccupation with compliance and control overshadows learning. Most students really have little at stake. Those who simply want to get by quickly learn that if they follow routines and do not cause trouble, they will pass and eventually graduate, regardless of the quality of their work. Few colleges, other than the most selective, demand more than a minimal level of attainment; students whose families can afford the tuition will generally find some college that will accept them.

Most American students who go directly into the work force after high school see few connections between achievement in school and the job market. They, along with their parents and potential employers, would be surprised to learn that European employers regularly examine high school transcripts and teacher recommendations when hiring. According to a recent survey by the National Federation of Independent Business, only 15 percent of U.S. employers follow this practice.[35]

## INCENTIVES FOR TEACHERS AND PRINCIPALS

Apart from the intrinsic satisfaction of doing a good job and the thanks of an occasional student, most teachers have few incentives for improving their own performance. Teachers do not receive additional pay for superior performance. Poor teachers are rarely disciplined or fired. Teacher compensation is almost always based on seniority and credentials beyond the bachelor's degree, even though neither of these has been shown to benefit student achievement in any systematic way. (Part of the reason may be that few districts require teachers to ensure that their additional course work is related to their subject specialty.) Teachers with the same seniority usually receive the same pay, regardless of their skills, special levels of competence, or the value of their skills on the open market.

Structuring an incentive system that can both attract and retain good teachers can be complex. Although starting salaries are important for attracting good teaching candidates, the better teachers appear to stay in the profession because of its intrinsic rewards. These same teachers often feel forced to leave teaching eventually because of low career salaries and poor working conditions.[36] One study comparing higher- and lower-quality teachers found the higher-quality group to be more interested in opportunities for professional growth and student achievement, willing to base pay on performance, impatient with seniority systems, and frustrated by bureaucratic demands for compliance and control. Not surprisingly, this study also found that such high-quality teachers were likely to leave teaching sooner than their less able counterparts.[37]

Increasing the capacity of teachers and principals to make decisions that directly affect the learning of students and the quality of the learning environment provides a set of intrinsic professional rewards that can offer powerful motivation to improve performance. But because school-site management places far greater responsibility for measurable results on teachers and principals, many might be reluctant to take on the extra burden without additional pay or other forms of compensation that reward such results.

**Pay for Performance: Individual Versus Group Rewards.** Individual merit pay has received the most attention in debates on how to improve teacher performance. But research indicates that individual merit pay may be a less effective performance incentive than group bonuses or nonmonetary professional rewards.[38] Even in business, where merit raises are standard practice, the trend is moving toward rewards based on the results of group effort.[39]

Researchers cite a number of reasons for the poor track record of individual merit pay. First, merit pay based on student achievement scores seems to motivate teachers to focus on prepping students for tests. Second, the competitive nature of most merit pay systems works against collegiality and teamwork among the faculty, two key characteristics of effective schools. Third, merit pay is usually awarded on the basis of supervisor evaluations. This situation creates adversarial relationships in which teachers try to hide problems from supervisors rather than work to solve them. Fourth, in order to avoid creating a divided faculty, principals tend to reward all teachers equally, defeating the intent of the program.[40] Group rewards, on the other hand, tend to promote greater collegiality, cooperation, and pooled effort.

**Professional Enhancement.** Most teachers do much the same work from their first day until retirement. A path of increasing professional responsibilities would provide an incentive to career-minded teachers and serve as a basis for differentiating salaries. Under the current system, teachers who wish to move up generally have to become administrators. With a career ladder, superior teachers who take on additional professional responsibilities in such areas as curriculum development or mentoring novice teachers become better-paid master teachers.

An important step in this direction has been taken with the establishment of the National

Board for Professional Teaching Standards, which has just begun to certify its first master teachers in a limited number of subject areas. Other areas will be added over the next several years as the certification process is thoroughly field-tested. The board has established high and rigorous standards for what experienced teachers should know and be able to do. In order to gain certification, teachers must thoroughly document over a period of months their classroom techniques, samples of student work, and evidence of subject mastery. They are also required to demonstrate the ability to effectively evaluate the work of novice teachers. This certification process is an independent, voluntary means of identifying highly accomplished teachers, and it is recognized by both national teachers' unions. As such, it could provide a legitimate basis for designating master teachers as part of a career ladder.

**If decentralization of school management is to result in increased accountability, we believe that school systems must reward teachers and administrators for performance, not merely for seniority and credentials. First, teacher salaries should be more sensitive to the prevailing regional labor market, paying higher rates to teachers in shortage areas, such as science and mathematics; those with specialized skills, such as expertise in technology or bilingual education; and those willing to work in distressed areas, such as the inner cities. Second, teachers and principals should be rewarded for improving the achievement of students.** Group bonuses, rather than individual merit pay, appear to provide a more effective tool for spurring schoolwide improvement within an atmosphere of collegiality. However, districts should experiment with different mixes of incentives to determine what works best for them, and incentive systems should be monitored for any unintended consequences that may arise.

Within the constraints of their resources, school systems should also make available a variety of professional rewards to individual high performers, such as expanded professional roles, sabbaticals, research grants, and summer internships at universities and businesses.

**Addressing Performance Problems.** Professional and financial rewards can help boost performance, but they are unlikely to improve performance that is barely adequate or unsatisfactory. When this is the case, intervention, designed to lead to either improvement or termination, is essential.

Identifying problem teachers and intervening can be very difficult in school systems where the teachers' and principals' unions and school boards are in constant opposition. School boards accuse unions of protecting incompetent teachers and administrators and often blame tenure rules for making it too difficult and costly to get rid of an incompetent veteran teacher or principal. Unions accuse school boards and the central administration of being unwilling to document problems and follow due process, and they point out that federal law obligates unions to represent any member of their bargaining unit in a disciplinary hearing, whether or not he or she is tenured.[41] As a result, in some districts, attempts to remove tenured teachers or principals have resulted in legal battles costly to both sides.

Tenure itself need not be an obstacle to weeding out incompetent teachers and administrators. Tenure was originally designed to protect teachers with proven abilities from arbitrary dismissal because they might hold unpopular views. But the granting of tenure should be a reward for good teaching, not a right based on seniority. School districts must take responsibility for the quality of their tenured teachers and administrators by maintaining selective hiring and promotion standards and a more effective evaluation system for both teachers and principals.

Outmoded evaluation systems based on the compliance-and-control model of management are a more serious obstacle to improving teacher performance. Supervisors may visit the classroom once or twice a year and are treated to a "model" lesson. They then evaluate the teacher's performance based on whether he or she has fulfilled a list of expected tasks. This approach to evaluation is fundamentally incompatible with the changing professional view of teachers as "managers of the learning process."

School boards and teachers' unions do not have to come to loggerheads on this issue. In a growing number of school districts, these two groups are working together to develop a more professional role for teachers. In these districts, peer review and coaching systems have become the dominant form of performance evaluation and appear to be working well.

Toledo, Ohio, is credited with being the first district to implement peer review. In 1981, the teachers' union negotiated a contract provision whereby the teachers themselves would police the ranks of veteran teachers in return for the right to review new teachers.[42] Under peer review, experienced teachers serve as mentors to new teachers and work with veterans who are having problems. The record of an intervention, demonstrating attempts at improvement, can become admissible evidence in a disciplinary or dismissal hearing.[43]

Many traditional unionists believe that peer review undermines union solidarity because it places one union member in judgment over another. However, research suggests that where peer review has been tried and has succeeded, it has not jeopardized the union but strengthened its professional role.[44] The success with peer review also shows that relationships between school boards and unions can be collaborative rather than adversarial. **We believe that peer review, peer coaching, and mentoring should be adopted more broadly as the most promising strategies for dealing with teacher performance problems.**

## INCENTIVES FOR STUDENTS

How can governance changes motivate students to work harder in school? Few reform strategies have acknowledged the critical need to have students take more responsibility for their own education.

Some students, of course, may not have access to quality schools or other learning resources, such as good libraries. We believe that states and communities should continue to strive to eliminate these inequities in educational opportunity. However, we also believe that if we wait for the elimination of all barriers to equal opportunity before we ask students to assume more personal responsibility for their own achievement, we will never reach our educational goals.

**Assessments, Certificates, and School Records.** Motivating students to become accountable for their own achievement means establishing some concrete incentives. Students need to know that their efforts in school have both immediate and long-range payoffs. We believe that performance-based assessments that have consequences for higher education or employment can provide a clear incentive for students to work harder in school. Performance-based assessments, grounded in high standards and rigorous academic content, should play an important role in the awarding of a high school diploma. This will make it a much more meaningful credential to both higher education institutions and businesses than it now is.

**We recommend the development of national performance-based assessments that provide an accurate reflection of a student's knowledge and ability to apply that knowledge. We further recommend that these should be used to provide students with meaningful educational credentials that qualify them for higher education, postsecondary training, and employment. In particular, we recommend that student eligibility for financial aid for college and training, including access to preferential student loans, be based at least in part on these assessments.***

**We urge the development of mastery certificates in a variety of academic and vocational areas to provide new incentives**

---

*See memorandum by PETER A. BENOLIEL (page 56).

to students, particularly those who are not college bound and who currently have few reasons to expend any effort in school. Employers should give hiring preference to high school graduates who have earned mastery certificates or who have other proof of good performance in high school, such as portfolios of schoolwork or transcripts showing grades.

Employers have been reluctant to use high school transcripts for hiring purposes because civil rights law requires employers to show that their criteria for hiring an individual will have a direct impact on job productivity, an often difficult and expensive task. The result is that the achievement of high school graduates is generally unknown to potential employers. Yet, there is good evidence that high school grades are a fairly good predictor of later job success because, in addition to mastery of subject matter, they indicate important work-related traits, such as dependability and perseverance.[45]

We believe that grades, teacher recommendations, and measures of conduct, such as attendance and discipline, provide important and useful information to employers and incentives for students. We therefore urge the courts, when interpreting civil rights laws, to recognize the public interest in allowing employers to make greater use of such information in hiring.

Another reason employers are reluctant to request high school transcripts is the slow response time of most schools.[46] We urge the schools to develop better information systems that will allow them to respond in a timely manner to employer requests for transcripts.

The Educational Testing Service (ETS) has developed a program to allow high school students, as early as the ninth grade, to build a computer record of their grades, test scores, awards and honors, teacher recommendations, and work experiences that can be accessed by employers. Called "Worklink," the program avoids legal obstacles partly because participation by students is voluntary.

**Career Training, Vocational Education, and the School-to-Work Transition.** Unlike other nations that maintain challenging standards in vocational and technical education, the United States does a poor job of designing, organizing, and delivering vocational and technical education for young adults not going on to college. For the most part, vocational education is still used as a dumping ground for students not considered fit for college.

In contrast, most of America's industrial competitors have well-developed systems of vocational, technical, and professional education to absorb the large numbers of students who do not attend a university.[47] In many of these nations, students who do well in school are first in line for an apprenticeship or a job upon graduation.

Apprenticeships and similar school-to-work programs that give preferential treatment to graduates based on their performance in school must satisfy a number of conditions if they are to provide a real incentive for students. Such programs must establish recognized vocational credentials, help correct real or perceived skill mismatches in the labor market, connect academic and applied learning, and provide meaningful work experiences. None of these conditions can be satisfied without a strong role for business. A business voice, especially in curriculum development and evaluation, provides guidance and legitimacy. In Germany, for example, the role of business is substantial. The government, industry, and the unions work together to determine the content of training at the work site.[48] Schools employ a permanent liaison to business, and employers help certify trainees. We urge greater collaboration between businesses and high schools to develop school-to-work programs that provide students with meaningful job skills and experience.

Although only a relatively small number of schools nationwide have implemented school-to-work transition programs, many program models exist.[49]

- **Career Academies.** These high school programs are designed around a specific career and offer structured work experiences. Each is a school within a school that provides a three- to four-year program integrating academic learning with the study of an industry and the careers of the people who work in it, such as health care or financial services. The Philadelphia High School Academies (see below) and the Academies of Finance in New York City are two excellent examples.

- **Tech Prep.** These programs link the last two years of high school with two years of community college, allowing students to train for a job while completing an academic program. Generally, these programs emphasize instruction in science and math as well as hands-on workplace applications. An extensive tech prep network is being pioneered by the state of Oregon. Boston's Project ProTech/Health Care and Project ProTech/Financial Services also provide good examples of this type of school-to-work program.

- **Youth Apprenticeships.** These programs use the workplace as a learning environment for developing both job-related and general workplace skills. Students "learn by doing" in paid employment and training supervised by expert adult mentors. Classroom vocational instruction and related courses that integrate academic and vocational learning are integral to the apprenticeship. A recognized occupational credential is awarded upon successful completion of the program. Most apprenticeship programs link secondary and postsecondary institutions in offering instruction (see page 27).

- **Occupational-Academic Cluster Programs.** These are generally large-scale programs offering all students in a high school a choice among several career pathways. Course work is clustered around general career areas (such as environment-related industries, manufacturing or service industries, and engineering). Students are usually exposed to a number of careers and may switch clusters. Academic studies and

## THE PHILADELPHIA HIGH SCHOOL ACADEMIES, INC.

Begun in 1969 through a collaboration of the Philadelphia Urban Coalition and the board of education, the Philadelphia High School Academies provide disadvantaged students with marketable job skills and improved prospects for employment upon graduation. There are now nine career academies operating in seventeen high schools. They range from the Electrical Academy at Thomas Edison High School to the Hotel, Restaurant, and Tourism Academy and the Academy of Law, Criminal Justice, and Public Administration.

Each of the academies represents an active partnership between business and the public schools. They are schools within schools that provide vocational education and career orientation while relating academics to the demands of a chosen occupational path. The school district provides academic and vocational teaching staff, equipment and supplies, facilities, and administrative support. The business community provides financial support, managerial expertise, advice on curriculum, paid work experience for in-school students, and job opportunities for graduates.

Each career academy is overseen by a board of governors, made up of industry representatives, that has responsibility for initiating budgets, approving expansion, and maintaining links with the private sector. The academy program will be expanding to more of Philadelphia's comprehensive high schools and expects to reach a total student enrollment of 5,000 by 1996.

## CORNELL YOUTH APPRENTICESHIP DEMONSTRATION PROJECT

The Cornell Youth Apprenticeship Demonstration Project is based on European models of apprenticeship, in which academic studies and vocational learning are integrated at the workplace. Six upstate New York school districts are participating in the project, which was begun by Cornell University's Department of Human Development and Family Studies. In the first year, 1991-92, twenty-two apprenticeship positions were provided in four companies. The apprenticeships are in three broad occupational areas: health care, manufacturing and engineering technology, and administration and office technology.

A coordinator at each school, advised by a committee representing teachers, counselors, administrators, apprentices, and parents, recruits students, arranges schedules, plans and conducts teacher in-service training, develops curriculum, and adapts instruction.

The program ensures that students are enrolled in courses appropriate to their apprenticeship, emphasizing college-preparatory academic courses. Special arrangements are made when specialized course work is required by the employer.

Learning at the work site is structured around specific technical and social skills, which are identified for each of the three broad occupational areas. An "Apprentice Progress Report" provides feedback to the student, the firm, and the schools. Employers pay students' salaries, and both they and the schools contribute staff time. The project provides consultation, in-service training, planning, coordination, and communication.

The program does not necessarily lead directly to employment after high school graduation. In fact, most of the first group have gone on to two- and four-year higher-education programs. However, almost all have mapped out career plans closely related to the area of their apprenticeship.

The program added twenty new apprenticeships in 1992-93 and thirty-one in 1993-94.

occupational instruction are integrated, and work-based experiences enable students to explore potential careers.

Evaluations of these programs have found a number of positive results: improved attitudes toward school and work, improved attendance, greater understanding of the connection between school and work, increased enrollment in science and math courses, and better jobs after graduation.[50]

In addition to these specific programs, the entire concept of vocational education is being rethought. CED's 1985 policy statement *Investing in Our Children* devoted considerable attention to the problems of vocational education. CED conducted research for that policy statement to determine the traits of entry-level workers valued most by employers. That study and subsequent research by the Department of Labor's Secretary's Commission on Achieving Necessary Skills (SCANS) identified general academic competence, positive attitudes and behaviors, and learning skills as most important for successful job performance. *Investing in Our Children* recommended that students be required to demonstrate an adequate level of academic achievement before being allowed to take occupationally specific training and that all vocational education majors be expected to complete a core academic curriculum.

The Interim Report of the National Assessment of Vocational Education, submitted to Congress in December 1993, found that few of the vocational education (voc-ed) reforms proposed in the 1980s have been implemented. Academic course work and homework are still minimal, and fewer than 40 percent of voc-ed graduates find jobs that match their training. An especially serious concern is the scattershot nature of most voc-ed programs. Only about a third of programs require students to concentrate on a particular occupational area, even though research indicates that such concentration increases the likelihood of finding a training-related job. **As a result, we reaffirm our previous recommendation that strong academic course work be a required component of all vocational programs. State policy makers and education officials should restructure all types of vocational education to emphasize academic competence along with career-specific training. Furthermore, like school-to-work programs, vocational programs should be designed in consultation with businesses to develop job skills required in the private sector.**

The Clinton Administration's School-to-Work Opportunities Act was recently signed into law. This act will help establish partnerships among employers, educators, and others to build a school-to-work system and will provide $300 million in venture capital to states and communities to design and implement a variety of apprenticeship, training, and vocational education programs. More than twenty states have submitted grant applications.[51]

# Chapter 3
# GOVERNING FOR RESULTS

Improved school management and accountability demand corresponding behavioral changes in the institutions and individuals that govern education. This chapter focuses on the institutions of governance and the individuals who run them, proposing what we believe will be practical solutions to the governance gridlock that now prevents meaningful reform.

Although the U.S. Constitution gives the states ultimate authority over education, the earliest impetus for establishing and operating schools grew out of the desire of local communities to educate their children. Massachusetts established the first state board of education in 1837 to assist local communities in delivering education, and this has served as a model for other states. Massachusetts also created the fiscal model for education funding in 1891, when it codified the arrangement making local districts responsible for setting budgets, selecting teachers, determining the curriculum, and providing the funds.[1]

Most Americans firmly believe in local control of public schools.[2] At the same time, decisions by local school boards on a number of issues are increasingly being challenged by parents. The causes of this ambivalence are not hard to find. School board attention to academic quality has lost out to contentious politics, micromanagement of day-to-day school operations, and divisive social issues. Even though the vast majority of boards conduct their business honestly, so many have been accused of patronage, corruption, and willful mismanagement that the reputation of the institution has suffered almost irreparable damage.

Some local school boards do provide good leadership. Such well-functioning boards are most common in communities that are homogeneous, have few funding problems, and have reached a consensus on educational goals and values.[3] The picture is much less positive in large urban and poor rural districts, where social problems are more intense, demographic changes are more rapid, poverty is more concentrated, politics are more divisive, and low achievement is more persistent.

The loss of confidence in local governance was reflected in the steady expansion of state government control over education during the 1980s. States have tried to raise educational standards by imposing accountability testing on teachers and students, reducing the resource gap between poor and affluent districts by increasing the state share of funding, and expanding state authority over local schools through takeovers of failing districts.

There is little reason to think that states are any better at governing schools than local school boards are. Much school reform has actually resulted from local initiatives in which the major state role was to provide seed money.[4] If anything, many state "reforms" of the 1980s have been responsible for some of the worst problems of local school governance. According to a study by the Center for Policy Research in Education (CPRE), most state reform packages have been incoherent and uncoordinated. The states have bombarded local districts with conflicting messages, forcing boards to make complicated decisions about the allocation of time and money.[5]

## REDUCING OVERREGULATION AND UNPRODUCTIVE MANDATES

Overregulation of schools is a serious problem that is severely straining local resources and limiting the ability of teachers and administrators to educate effectively. *Educational* regulations, such as maximum class size, mandated school time spent on a particular subject, and centralized textbook adoption, dictate how schools can and cannot use their instructional resources, limiting flexibility to develop distinctive educational programs. Equally troubling are *social* mandates, sometimes funded, often not. It seems that whenever a social crisis, such as AIDS, child abuse, or drunk driving, is perceived, the government looks to the schools to solve it.

Of course, some mandates are necessary. The government mandates that public schools not discriminate on the basis of race, ethnicity, or gender, a requirement that is fundamental to our system of free public education. Basic health and safety regulations are essential. Some mandates are legitimate and effective policy tools to create positive change in schools.

But mandates, especially when unfunded, are a political temptation for legislators. Even when budgets are tight, politicians can garner political credit by creating new programs, passing laws to protect children from some per-

## REEVALUATING COSTLY MANDATES

Mandates are imposed on schools and districts by a variety of sources, including state and federal governments and teachers' and administrators' unions. Mandates can be legislated, or they can be imposed by interpretations of statutes made by the courts or regulatory agencies. They can also be explicitly drawn into contracts. The following are some examples of mandates from a variety of sources that can inhibit school effectiveness.

### A CURRENT EXAMPLE: SPECIAL EDUCATION AND FULL INCLUSION

The current movement toward full inclusion of disabled students in regular classrooms may be one of the most educationally disruptive mandated situations facing local districts. The federal Individuals with Disabilities Education Act requiring placement of disabled students in "the least restrictive environment" has led courts and state education departments, largely on social rather than on educational grounds, to require local districts to integrate many special education students into regular classrooms, no matter how severe their physical, mental, or emotional handicaps.

Although mainstreaming of some learning-disabled and physically handicapped children is desirable, at least in part because too many students have been misidentified as disabled and suffered educational harm as a result, not all special education students benefit from this mandate, and some may receive less educational attention than before. Students who need special medical services or who have severe emotional problems can place an undue burden on teachers lacking specialized training and can impede the academic progress of the rest of the class.

Much of the increase in per-pupil costs in the past twenty years can be traced to the rapid growth in special education.* In Los Angeles, for example, instructional expenditures for disabled students grew 147 percent in the 1980s, while general education spending grew 46 percent. It now costs Los Angeles an average of $11,500 to educate each special education student, compared with $4,000 for the nondisabled.** Some districts see mainstreaming as an easy way to cut the escalating costs of special education, despite the possible consequences for both students and teachers. However, if mainstreaming is to be of real benefit, a sufficient range of special education support services should be available, and these will continue to be costly.

### FEDERAL MANDATES

**Compensatory Education (ESEA Title I).** Most Title I funds come with strict targeting rules

ceived danger, or requiring instruction in the latest social trend, often without undertaking the unpopular task of paying for the new requirement. If programs fail or become very costly, others can be blamed for poor implementation or mismanagement.[6] As a result, legislative or governing authorities often give little thought to how local school districts will fund a new requirement or how new mandates will reduce the time and resources available for academic study. In addition, school boards and central administrators often hide behind these mandates as an excuse to avoid dealing with their own inefficient use of resources. Even though most mandates are well intentioned, those that are misdirected can seriously harm the very students they aim to protect.

We propose the following principles that can guide legislators and education governance bodies in evaluating mandates:

- All mandates should be evaluated for their broad educational benefits and their cost in money, personnel, and time.

- Mandates should be evaluated on whether they unduly limit the flexibility of the schools to meet the learning needs of their students.

which effectively require that schools educate their disadvantaged children in pull-out programs. Teachers and principals have very little leeway to determine if children's needs can be better met in other settings.

**Asbestos Abatement.** The Asbestos Hazard Education Act required all local education agencies to inspect for asbestos, develop management plans, and in many cases, do extensive abatement work. This federal mandate has cost some school districts millions of dollars, with little or no federal funding. Although in many cases asbestos abatement may have been needed, this mandate failed to take into account any economies of scale to be gained from federal or state technical assistance, leaving district administrators with no expertise to address the problem.

STATE AND DISTRICT MANDATES

**Credit-Hour Graduation Requirements.** In the 1980s, increasing numbers of states instituted credit-hour graduation requirements for local schools. These mandates inhibit school flexibility to experiment with integrated curricula, class-period arrangements, or other reorganizations of the school day. Some evidence suggests schools simply watered down class curricula to allow more students to meet the new time requirements.

**Excessive Documentation.** Some of the most expensive and time-consuming mandates are excessive process regulations established to enforce everything from appropriate teacher placements, planning processes, and course offerings to class size. For example, the New York City standard operating procedures manual spells out in forty-six pages all the rules that must be mastered and followed before a check can be written for even minimal amounts.

UNION CONTRACTS

**Strict Restrictions on Teachers' Time.** Some union contracts spell out work rules in great detail, such as length of lunch breaks, length and schedule of the workday, and the maximum number of times principals can call for meetings with teachers. Such restrictions limit schools' flexibility to meet individual and changing student needs.

*U.S. Department of Education, *Digest of Education Statistics, 1992* (Washington, D.C.: U.S. Government Printing Office, 1992), p. 64; James A. Tucker, "Focus on Special Education, Yesterday, Today, and Tomorrow," in Teresa Bunsen, et. al., eds., *Forum on Emerging Trends in Special Education: Implications for Personnel Preparation*, ed. Teresa Bunsen et al. Washington, D.C., April; 9-10, 1992, (Greeley, Col.: Division of Special Education, University of North Colorado-Greeley, 1992).

**Janet R. Beales, *Special Education: Expenditures and Obligations*, no. 24, (Los Angeles: Reason Foundation, 1993).

- Mandates directed at procedures or other educational inputs, rather than achievement, should be regarded with suspicion.

- In general, governing bodies should not impose expensive social or safety mandates unless they are willing to substantially fund them.

- When adopted, mandates should be cost-effective.

"Reevaluating Costly Mandates" (see pages 30 and 31) gives examples of some current educational mandates that do not measure up particularly well against these criteria.

## IMPROVING THE LEADERSHIP OF LOCAL SCHOOL BOARDS

We strongly support local control over schools, but we believe that the current goals and activities of local school boards need to be significantly changed. The bottom line is higher student achievement. What school boards *do* to achieve that goal is more important than how they are structured. Those who govern must provide their schools with a policy and resource environment that will allow teachers and students to concentrate on learning. Within that framework, there is a good deal of room for states and local school districts to experiment with alternative forms of governance and school management to determine what will work best in a specific community.

Earlier in this statement (pages 5 and 6), we listed what we believe are the essential governing responsibilities of education at all levels. This list is especially pertinent for local school boards. Too many boards neglect these broader responsibilities and instead try to micromanage the day-to-day operations of the schools. Not only is this unproductive; it generally causes managerial weakness and demoralization because decisions made by superintendents or by school management committees are then second-guessed at board meetings. It is no wonder that superinten-

dents average less than six years on the job and that big-city superintendents average only two and a half years.[7]

Although school boards have always had a political function, the last few decades have witnessed an explosion of special interests vying for representation on boards and looking out for the needs of their constituents at the expense of the majority of students. As school board politics have become more divisive, representation from the community has also changed. Although some of this change, such as greater representation of previously excluded groups, is positive, some is not. The trend toward having single-member electoral districts for school boards rather than electing at-large community members has heightened this divisiveness. Fewer business and civic leaders of stature are willing to volunteer for what they now perceive as an unproductive, frustrating, and thankless task.[8]

### BUILDING POLICY BOARDS

**Local school boards should abandon their penchant for micromanagement and concentrate on educational policy.** The policy board should be responsible for making decisions in the broad policy areas outlined on pages 5 and 6, the superintendent should be responsible for seeing that policies are carried out, and the individual schools should have the authority to manage their own day-to-day operations. We endorse the framework presented by The Twentieth Century Fund, in its recent report on school governance, to guide the actions of education policy boards.[9] Policy boards should:

- Establish overall objectives for curriculum but not be involved in curriculum development

- Establish policies for contracting and purchasing and hire independent auditors to review the execution of these policies but not themselves supervise these arrangements

- Establish staff-development policies to improve teaching in the district

- Work alongside general-purpose government to ensure that educational policies are coordinated with a variety of children's services

## IMPROVING THE CALIBER OF SCHOOL BOARD MEMBERS

Changing the nature of local school boards is only half the battle. The other half is improving the caliber of the individuals who serve on the boards.

Of America's nearly 16,000 school boards, the majority are democratically elected; the rest are appointed through a variety of mechanisms. Elected school boards are often criticized for attracting individuals who are poorly versed in educational matters, are more interested in using school board membership as a stepping-stone to higher political office, have an ideological ax to grind, or see school board service as an opportunity for financial gain or patronage.[10] Unfortunately, there is no evidence that appointed boards are any better or worse at avoiding these problems.

Public apathy is one of the greatest obstacles to improving the caliber of school board members. Average voter turnout for school board elections ranges from 5 to 15 percent. Few citizens without children in the schools take any active interest in school governance; they consider the education system only as taxpayers when the budget or a bond issue is up for approval. In addition, many school board elections are held at different times from general elections and tend to be poorly publicized. Although school board and general elections were originally separated to distance the schools from local politics, this "protection" appears counterproductive. Higher voter turnout is needed to protect school systems from special interests and ideological factions. **We recommend that districts hold school board elections at the same time as general elections.**

Another serious problem is the almost complete lack of training for school board members. School systems are complex organizations. A typical school board in a medium-size urban district of 50,000 students has to manage a budget of many millions of dollars, has upward of 5,000 employees working at dozens of sites, has to serve tens of thousands of meals a day, and often oversees the largest transportation operation in the area.[11] School boards must also make decisions within highly public and political forums.

Despite these considerable responsibilities, training and development for local school boards is inadequate at best. Although individual board members may take part in actitivites organized by their state associations, little attention is paid in most states to developing boards as governing bodies.[12]

We believe that better training for current and prospective school board members is essential to improving the capacity of boards to lead. **The states should work with organizations that have both expertise and self-interest, such as the National School Boards Association and their state affiliates, to develop training programs both for individual board members and for boards as a whole in such critical areas as defining responsibilities, delegating authority, managing finances, and resolving conflict.** An extensive initiative of this type has been undertaken by the California School Boards Association with help from the National School Boards Association (see page 34). Some communities have created nonpartisan screening committees of leading citizens whose job it is to identify a pool of potential school board members, evaluate their qualifications, and in many cases, support a reform slate.

Another interesting proposal for improving school board leadership is requiring prospective board members to run on a slate that presents an agreed-upon program for the district's schools (see page 35). This may be an effective strategy for communities in which factionalism and political infighting have paralyzed the school board. This approach would induce school boards to work as teams with a program for learning and achievement instead of concentrating on distracting political and social issues. Voters, in turn, would clearly understand what the school board planned to achieve and could more easily hold it accountable.

However, school board reform in itself is not enough; the states must play a decisive part in framing the roles and responsibilities of boards. **States should provide legislative guidance on the appropriate roles of school boards in accomplishing their primary mission of academic achievement.**

Accountability must be enhanced in all school board restructuring and reform. Parents, citizens, and educators need to know who is responsible for the financial health of the schools, the educational direction the schools are taking, and the results they are achieving.

## SUPERINTENDENTS AND SCHOOL BOARDS

As the relationship between school boards and schools changes, the role of the superintendent appointed by the school board to oversee the district must also change. The superintendent is the chief executive officer of the school district, with the responsibility for producing good student achievement within reasonable budget constraints. In fact, as the lack of results and the fiscal problems of public education have become more pronounced, a few districts, such as Minneapolis and Milwaukee, have gone outside the traditional educational community to hire school superintendents from business or with public finance experience.

Greater fiscal accountability is critical, and we support, in principle, looking outside traditional educational channels for school superintendents. Nevertheless, we believe that the superintendent of schools must be more than just a good fiscal or organizational manager; he or she must be first and foremost an educational leader who establishes a clear sense of purpose centered on academic attainment. In a restructured education system based on flexibility and accountability for results, it is the superintendent's responsibility to implement the policies established by the local board and state educational authorities and to provide the support systems needed by the indi-

## TRAINING CALIFORNIA SCHOOL BOARDS

The California School Boards Association (CSBA) is launching a two-year project to address the problems of school board governance identified by a task force formed by the National School Boards Association and chaired by the executive director of the CSBA. To help define the increasingly complex expectations and duties faced by local school boards, the task force created four categories of responsibilities: (1) setting the vision for the district, (2) establishing a supportive structure and appointing the superintendent, (3) ensuring accountability (fiscal and programmatic), and (4) engaging in advocacy on behalf of children and the public schools. The CSBA is trying to put the recommendations of the national task force into action by developing a comprehensive training curriculum for school boards that focuses on both the importance of how a board governs and the decisions it makes.

Some of the basic characteristics of effective board members that CSBA's training will promote are: an understanding of the duties of board members, especially the leadership role that connects the community and school system; valuing teamwork; demonstrating respect for the district's programs, staff, colleagues, and constituents by listening and providing public support; creating trust within the board and district through open and honest communication about expectations and desires; concentrating on outcomes, not procedures; behaving professionally and taking membership seriously; and establishing equitable and consistent policies and programs.

## CREATING CHARTER SCHOOL BOARDS

Creating charter school systems, not just individual charter schools, is the radical, grassroots approach to school governance reform advocated by Phillip Schlechty and Robert Cole of the Center for Leadership in School Reform, Louisville, Kentucky. Schlechty and Cole propose a solution to the ineffectual politicking that dominates many local school boards and takes away the boards' ability to work for positive change in schools. They call for electing all school board members at the same time and as a slate, rather than the current practice of staggering the election of individual members. This would provide an important measure of stability to policy, planning, and implementation. In addition, individuals would be less vulnerable to special-interest group politics.

School boards are criticized for not having an educational vision to guide their decisions; but charter school boards, like charter schools, would have to commit themselves publicly to an educational philosophy and provide a detailed description of their long-term goals and strategies for the school district and how they plan to implement them. With several slates running for election, voters could see different possibilities for their schools laid out and debated, enabling them to better determine a board's ability to govern. Slate members also would have to be representative of the whole community, including the different racial and ethnic groups and geographic regions.

Schlechty and Cole recommend electing slates for at least four years, possibly up to ten years, in order to allow for a board's efforts to take hold. However, the board would be overseen by a government body with recall power so that voters could get rid of a board in the case of misconduct or misrepresentation.

---

vidual schools so that they can best carry out their academic mission. To do this, superintendents must have a clear understanding of what makes learning happen in the classroom.

The superintendent is usually the most visible education leader in the community, as well as the primary target for public dissatisfaction with the schools. Therefore, one of the superintendent's most important roles is to rally support from the public, not only from parents with children in the schools but also from the growing proportion of nonparents, whose support for school funding is essential. As part of this very visible role, the superintendent is also the best individual liaison to the variety of community health, social, and recreational services that are needed by the district's schoolchildren.

A good working relationship between the superintendent and the school board is fundamental for educational success. But research by the Institute for Educational Leadership shows that local boards are, in general, not very good at dealing with conflicts with their superintendents or evaluating a superintendent's performance.[13] The high turnover among superintendents, especially in urban districts, underscores this serious problem. This is an area in which improved board development and training are particularly important.

## BUILDING COMMUNITY SUPPORT

The most effective school boards are those that have a mandate from the larger community. Without strong, ongoing community leadership, educators may be defeated by public apathy (and, in some cases, hostility). **We believe that leaders from all sectors of the community—business, foundations, civic and religious institutions, and the media—must work actively to convince the public that the primary mission of the schools is learning and achievement. While doing so, they must also emphasize the responsibility of the broader community to meet the social and health needs of children.**

A number of states and communities have helped raise public awareness and support for public school reform through major media and grassroots campaigns. To win support of the electorate for South Carolina's statewide school-restructuring effort, the South Carolina business community mounted a successful statewide media campaign and sponsored town meetings to discuss the changes.

In 1991, the Omaha Chamber of Commerce took the lead in creating the Omaha 2000 initiative to rally support for the public schools, early childhood education, and workplace readiness. Omaha 2000 spent its first year developing a community consensus on the problems facing education and in its second year implemented an action plan designed around the National Education Goals. Omaha 2000 is issuing detailed annual reports on the progress being made on each goal.

At the national level, The Business Roundtable, the Department of Education, and the Advertising Council have marshaled a broad coalition of corporations and education organizations to sponsor a public-service campaign in support of quality public education.

**We urge business, government, civic leaders, and the media in every community to mount a vigorous and sustained communications campaign to rally the public to support the efforts of their schools.**

## THE STATE ROLE IN IMPROVING EDUCATION GOVERNANCE

In the early 1980s, governors and state legislatures began to take a much more aggressive role in setting the education reform agenda. Governors provided critical national leadership on a number of key education issues.

Virtually all state constitutions guarantee their citizens some variation of an "adequate and efficient education," but almost all states delegate most governing responsibility to local school districts. Nevertheless, states retain the constitutional authority to change that arrangement; they can bypass or even eliminate school boards if they wish. A growing number of states are allowing some public schools to negotiate a charter directly with the state and bypass the local school district (see page 17 for a discussion of charter schools).

We do not believe that overseeing the operation of individual schools is the best role for the state. State government is far too removed to provide effective oversight for schools in vastly different communities with greatly differing needs. The programs of individual schools need to be coordinated with those of other schools that serve a common geographic area and similar population, so that children can make smooth transitions between schools and from elementary to middle and high school. Equally important, individual schools need to be linked with other community institutions, such as libraries, museums, and after-school centers, to connect students to the widest variety of learning opportunities and resources. Finally, some type of local coordinating mechanism is needed to link schools with health and social services for children in a way that does not place additional nonacademic burdens on the schools.

**We believe that the primary state role in education governance is to establish broad educational goals and to ensure that local authorities, whether at the community or the school level, have the support services, resources, and oversight to attain those goals.** We believe that states should concentrate on the following functions and tasks:

- Establishing rigorous academic content and performance standards and assessments consistent with national standards and assessments

- Establishing standards for teaching credentials and upgrading teacher preparation and professional development

- Reducing needless and costly mandates on local districts and schools in exchange for performance agreements from districts or schools

- Providing legislative guidance to localities on the appropriate roles and responsibilities of school boards

- Establishing collaboration among agencies serving children's social welfare and health needs and between these agencies and the schools

- Providing oversight to ensure local district accountability and intervening, if necessary, with failing districts

- Revising school finance formulas and methods of raising revenue to ensure that resources are adequate to meet the educational needs of all the state's children, especially the disadvantaged

Currently, state education departments dedicate a large portion of their resources and personnel to ensuring compliance with federal mandates. As state education departments transform themselves from compliance-and-control agencies into service-and-support agencies, we urge them to ensure that resources are not simply added to accommodate new functions and personnel without first eliminating functions and personnel that are duplicative or no longer necessary.

## SETTING PERFORMANCE STANDARDS

Although we believe strongly in national standards and assessments, we also believe that each state should set its own expectations for student performance, which may be higher than the national standards. But in their rush to create *outcomes-based* education systems, many states are creating a dizzying array of fuzzy, nonacademic goals that are overly subjective and highly controversial. In many cases, even the academic goals are too vague to serve as true performance standards.

In Ohio, an outcomes-based education plan was defeated in the legislature because of strong objections to unmeasurable goals requiring students to demonstrate that they are environmentally responsible and are able to function in a multicultural society.

Among Pennsylvania's fifty-five "learner outcomes" are such nonacademic goals as "all students should know and use, when appropriate, community health resources." Although it may be important for children to develop this skill, it is questionable whether the school is the appropriate institution to teach it. Kentucky's Learning Goals and Expectations contain such vague statements as "students will make sense of the variety of materials they read . . . the various things they observe . . . and the various messages to which they listen" without defining what "make sense of" might mean. Kentucky also expects students to "demonstrate strategies for becoming and remaining mentally and emotionally healthy," with no indication of how this is to be achieved or measured.

**Policy makers should firmly reject vague or values-laden goals that cannot be measured.** This does not mean that values have no place in our schools. On the contrary, schools should be very conscious about the messages they send students concerning conduct, discipline, honesty, self-worth, reliability, fairness, and respect for others. By establishing positive school climates and clear codes of conduct, schools help shape their students' values and their readiness to take their places in the adult world. Moreover, quite apart from their larger societal effects, such attitudes and behaviors help schools fulfill their educational mission. Parents, employers, and the larger community must actively support the schools' efforts in this area.

## BUILDING COLLABORATIVE RELATIONSHIPS

State governments must bring new coherence to the balkanized maze of policies, programs, and agencies that serve children's social and health needs. Although we normally would caution against creating new government agencies, some states may need to establish some type of umbrella authority to lift the social welfare burden off the backs of school personnel.

Such authority would ensure that children's services, including education, are appropriately coordinated and effectively linked. This would clearly vest responsibility for meeting children's noninstructional needs with the larger community so that teachers could teach. Where appropriate, services could be provided in the school building but would not be the direct responsibility of the school.[14] New Mexico has developed a new framework for service delivery based on common goals for all agencies that serve children, chief among them "helping each child achieve success in school." To make this strategy work, New Mexico is establishing new local governance mechanisms to provide local input and accountability.[15]

## OVERSIGHT AND INTERVENTION FOR ACCOUNTABILITY

When school districts consistently fail to educate their students or are clearly mismanaging resources, states have no choice but to intervene. States are increasingly exercising their power to declare "educational bankruptcy" for failing school systems, as New Jersey did several years ago with Jersey City. We fully support states' use of educational receivership as a tool of last resort. However, we believe it is far better for states to develop strategies for identifying and correcting educational problems before they get out of hand. We urge states to develop oversight mechanisms that will help keep local districts focused on their educational priorities. One

---

### NEW YORK STATE'S "SCHOOL QUALITY REVIEW"

As part of its "A New Compact for Learning," New York State just completed its second year of piloting a new assessment process called the "School Quality Review." Modeled on the school inspectorate system in England, the School Quality Review is designed to support and strengthen schools in three ways: (1) by establishing an ongoing "culture of review" or inquiry within individual schools, (2) by helping schools increase student achievement by improving the quality of teaching and learning, and (3) by fostering public support for schools by increasing public confidence in them.

The reviews are conducted by teams consisting primarily of currently practicing teachers and administrators from other districts, as well as parents and representatives of the school community. This external review is meant to complement an active and ongoing self-review by the school in question. The average size of the review teams is twelve, although this may vary. Each team has a senior reviewer, who is a current or recently retired principal or experienced teacher. Different members of the review team are asked to

review different aspects of school performance, with the most important being teaching and learning. The team is managed by a representative of the New York State Department of Education.

The review team spends about one week at the school, shadowing students, reviewing portfolios of student work, observing teachers, attending school meetings, and interviewing administrators and parents. At the end of the week, the review team presents a collective oral evaluation for the school staff; this is followed up with an official written report.

Although at this stage in developing the School Quality Review there are no official consequences for schools that are reviewed, the state plans to use the results of these reviews to develop practice standards that can become the basis of a broader accountability system for its schools. Nevertheless, participating schools are finding the reviews to be immediately helpful. These schools report that the review has helped focus their attention on teaching and learning and that they have used the results to develop more effective educational plans.

such initiative, the "School Quality Review," is currently under way in seventy-five school districts in New York State as part of the state's "A New Compact for Learning" (see page 38).

## ADEQUATE SCHOOL FUNDING

One of the most difficult and contentious issues facing state governance of education is the inadequacy of resources in some poor school districts, often in the face of gross disparities between districts. In some states, the per-pupil expenditure in the highest-spending districts is more than two and a half times that in the lowest.[16] These wide disparities in school funding are the result of a governance system that assigns to local communities a large portion of the responsibility for financing their own public schools. As a result of earlier efforts to reduce funding inequities, states have assumed a larger proportion of school financing in the past two decades. For the nation as a whole, states and localities now share the burden almost equally, at about 47 percent each, with a small federal contribution (see Figure 1). Localities raise most of their revenues through the property tax; state funding comes primarily from general revenues.

About half the states are currently in the process of rethinking or redesigning their school-funding systems. Few states have taken the initiative on this vital issue themselves; most state efforts have been driven by court orders resulting from lengthy litigation. Many of these court-driven reforms have tried to minimize resource disparities among districts, often by increasing funding in low-spending districts and at times capping spending in wealthy districts.

We generally support state efforts to increase resources for schools with clearly demonstrable funding inadequacies, especially those with large numbers of children who have special needs. These schools will undoubtedly need, for example, better teachers, books, equipment, or facilities to improve their educational performance.

But money alone will not remedy the serious educational deficiencies in most of our schools. In fact, overall real educational expenditures have grown about 80 percent in the last two decades with no significant improvement in school performance (see Figure 2, page 40).[17] Although some of this financial increase is attributable to increasing social mandates and the growth in special education, much of it is not. Many low-performing districts have high per-pupil expenditures but make poor use of their funds. Research on school effectiveness (see Chapter 2) suggests that changes in school organization that emphasize academic performance and the more effective use of resources are the ingredients most needed to improve student achievement.

Although there have been vigorous empirical and methodological debates about whether additional educational resources raise student achievement, the evidence appears consistent with our view: *Money matters, not across-the-board, but only if schools are organized to use it effectively to promote achievement.*[18]

**Quality Schools at Reasonable Cost.** Educational, social, and other mandates from federal, state, and local governments currently prescribe how local districts and schools must use many of their resources. These mandates severely limit the use of resources in ways that best meet the needs of students. In some districts, considerable funds are diverted from direct educational uses to central district

## Figure 1

### Percent of Total Revenues for U.S. K-12 Education, by Source, 1960 to 1990

| Government Level | 1960 | 1970 | 1980 | 1990 |
|---|---|---|---|---|
| Federal | 4.4% | 8.0% | 9.8% | 6.1% |
| State | 39.1 | 39.9 | 46.8 | 47.2 |
| Local/Other | 56.5 | 52.1 | 43.3 | 46.6 |

SOURCE: *Digest of Education Statistics, 1992,* (Washington, D.C.: U.S. Department of Education, 1992), p. 150.

Figure 2

## Primary and Secondary Education U.S. Total and Current Expenditures* per Pupil, 1950 to 1993 (in nominal and real 1992-93 dollars)

|      | Total Expenditures Per Pupil | | | Current Expenditures Per Pupil | | |
|------|-------------------|----------------------------|------------------------------------------------|-------------------|----------------------------|------------------------------------------------|
|      | Nominal Dollars | Real 1992-93 Dollars | Average Annual Real Percent Change** | Nominal Dollars | Real 1992-93 Dollars | Average Annual Real Percent Change** |
| 1950 | $260 | $1,567 | — | $210 | $1,266 | — |
| 1960 | 471 | 2,285 | 3.84% | 375 | 1,820 | 3.70% |
| 1970 | 955 | 3,603 | 4.66 | 816 | 3,079 | 5.40 |
| 1980 | 2,491 | 4,573 | 2.41 | 2,272 | 4,171 | 3.10 |
| 1990 | 5,532 | 6,210 | 3.11 | 4,962 | 5,570 | 2.93 |
| 1993 | 6,405 | 6,405 | 1.04 | 5,721 | 5,721 | 0.90 |

* Expenditures per pupil in average daily attendance. Total expenditures are current expenditures plus capital outlay and interest on school debt.

** Rates of change are compounding.

SOURCE: U.S. Department of Education, *Digest of Education Statistics, 1993* (Washington, D.C.: U.S. Government Printing Office, 1993), p. 164.

administration, nonacademic services, and nonteaching personnel. Both interstate and interdistrict analyses of staffing patterns have found that as spending increases, increasing proportions go to nonteaching staff.[19]

A particularly striking example is Washington, D.C., one of the highest-spending districts in the country, where the public school system of 181 schools and 81,000 students is supported by a central administration of 1,250.[20] Although not strictly comparable, the district's Catholic school system provides a striking contrast. The Catholic Archdiocese of Washington runs a system of 102 schools and 29,849 students with a central administration staff of only 15 people.[21]

Undoubtedly, a substantial portion of the increase in noninstructional spending is being used for important social and health services for children. Nevertheless, costs can be cut substantially by reducing unnecessary central administration and school-level noninstructional staff. In appropriate instances, these funds can then be redirected to meet the instructional needs of the children. **School boards and superintendents have the responsibility to ensure that sufficient funds get to the classroom to improve learning. We believe that state governments should monitor district spending to ensure that funds get to the school and, specifically, to the classroom.**

A study of the Union Township, New Jersey, school system, conducted by Deloitte &

has also decided to end dependence on the property tax. States have different tax preferences and must make revenue-raising decisions in the context of their own overall tax systems. However, the movement to sales and excise taxes tends to shift funding responsibility for schools to the less affluent; it eliminates the implicit federal subsidization of education by shifting from a revenue source that is tax deductible on federal income taxes to one that is not; and it designates revenue sources less stable than the property tax to support education.

The second issue, community support, is primarily political and demographic. It is determined by the public's overall affluence, its perception of the educational value it gets for its expenditures, and the proportion of voters who feel they have a stake in quality education. In recent years, voters have repeatedly rejected school budgets and new bond issues to support schools. In this climate, increases in education spending will require restored public confidence in the ability of schools to use resources effectively to increase student learning.

Whether educational funding increases, decreases, or remains the same, we must answer the fundamental question: Who should pay for schools? Overburdened urban and poor rural school districts may be unable to finance as large a share of their school systems as wealthier suburbs.

**States have the ultimate responsibility to ensure that all schools have adequate resources from their combined funding sources to reach desired levels of educational achievement. However, in view of the benefits that individuals and their local communities receive from education, we believe that all local districts should carry a reasonable share of school financing.** State and local shares should be based on an assessment of local ability to pay relative to other districts in the state.

Much discussion and litigation on school financing have focused on funding disparities rather than on whether funding is adequate to achieve desired educational goals. Of course, in some situations, reforms that reduce disparities may also make funding more adequate for poorer schools, as in the recent Michigan shift from local property taxes to the state sales tax as a primary revenue source. This is often not the case, however, and a genuine adequacy standard provides no justification for ceilings on local educational spending. Under an adequacy standard, there is no reason to limit local revenues for schools. Furthermore, such limits may well have negative consequences; limiting local spending on public education may cause parents to abandon the public schools.[25] Should this occur to any appreciable degree, the middle-class constituency for public education could decline further, making access to tax revenues increasingly difficult. **Although states should ensure that local schools have adequate funds, they should also allow local communities to raise additional funds and to make allocation decisions concerning these funds.**

## THE FEDERAL ROLE IN EDUCATION GOVERNANCE

The federal government has traditionally played only a minor role in elementary and secondary education. But federal actions have an impact on educational decision making at the state and local levels out of proportion to the actual level of federal funding. Although the federal government provides only about 6 percent of all public school funding, the rules and regulations that go with this funding can have a strong influence on state and local education policies and practices.

Historically, the federal government has focused most of its attention and funding on programs addressing the educational needs of the disadvantaged and of handicapped students. In addition, the federal government supports educational research and various other targeted programs in science and mathematics education.

With the recent passage of the Goals 2000: Educate America Act, the federal government has created a valuable new platform from which to promote academic excellence. Goals 2000 creates a framework for establishing and implementing national standards for what students should know and be able to do, assessments based on those standards, and incentives for achieving them (see Appendix 1). The act also provides grants to states and localities for designing improvement plans that will help all students meet challenging academic standards. Finally, it establishes a National Skills Standards Board to stimulate development of a voluntary national system of work force skills standards.

The Goals 2000: Educate America Act provides important incentives to create a set of challenging academic standards for all students. **We strongly believe that school effectiveness should be judged by whether students can meet challenging national content and performance standards in a variety of core academic subjects. We believe that these standards should apply to students in all parts of the country. We also support national assessments to determine whether students are, in fact, attaining these standards.**

**Students should be required to demonstrate academic proficiency in order to earn a high school diploma, be eligible for admittance to college, and receive financial aid. We also support national achievement examinations that can be used to provide students with certificates of mastery in a variety of academic and vocational subjects.** (See the discussion of "student incentives," page 24).

The federal government should continue to upgrade the effectiveness of its current programs to support implementation of Goals 2000 at the state and local levels and ensure that all federal education policies and programs are coherent and coordinated.

## FEDERAL PROGRAMS

**Assistance to the Disadvantaged.** Title I is by far the federal government's largest single precollege education program. Its 1993 appropriation was $6.7 billion, or three-quarters of the total federal spending on primary and secondary education. Unfortunately, Title I funds do not always reach the neediest children and schools, do not significantly raise student achievement, and as currently configured, may actually inhibit important school reforms.

The major problems with Title I are its inflexible design and the fact that funds are spread so thin that many children in high-poverty, low-achieving schools receive no assistance. Fourteen percent of schools with poverty rates of 50 percent and higher receive no Title I assistance, whereas almost half of schools with less than 10 percent poor children receive funds. This situation occurs despite the fact that Title I students in low-poverty schools perform at higher levels than the average student in high-poverty schools. **We urge Congress to allocate more Title I funds to schools with high concentrations of poverty.**

Although Title I has been credited with helping to narrow the basic skills gap between minority and white children, it has been largely ineffective in closing the gap or promoting higher-order learning skills. This suggests that Title I funds are not being used effectively.

At the heart of this problem are the inflexible rules that force most schools to use the funds for *pull-out programs*, which take students out of their regular classrooms. Although there are some good pull-out programs, there is also evidence to conclude that schoolwide strategies, such as Accelerated Schools and "Success for All" (see page 12), can be more effective at boosting achievement. Currently, Title I allows schools with poverty rates over 75 percent to use their funds for schoolwide improvement. However, this provision is being utilized by only a small proportion of eligible schools. Many principals of eligible schools report a lack of information about these provisions. **We support proposals to expand flexible use of Title I** funds for schoolwide improvement by lowering the poverty threshold for schools and improving information about the program. To ensure that the funds are being effectively employed, schools should be required to show how Title I funds are to be used in their long-range educational investment plans or performance contracts.

Neither increased funds nor greater flexibility in their use will be effective unless the perverse financial incentives of the Title I program are eliminated. Because schools receive funds from their districts based on their number of low-achieving children, they lose money when student achievement improves. Schools therefore have an incentive for children to fail. We believe the criteria for allocating Title I funds should not be tied to the numbers of low-achieving students in a school.

Other Categorical Programs. Strict accounting rules often inhibit schools from combining funds from different programs, even where there is an overlap among the children served. For example, 35 percent of limited English proficiency (LEP) students are in Title I programs, and 15 percent of Title I students are LEP students. We believe the federal government should allow schools to combine funding from different categorical programs as long as the school is held accountable for using them for the objectives intended and this intended use is clearly delineated in the school's educational investment plan.

Coordinating Children's Services. Actual coordination of children's services with education is best accomplished at the state and local levels. But the federal government can set the pace by bringing greater coherence to its own programs and policies for children and by giving states and localities more flexibility in the use of federal funding for these programs.

Several pieces of recently passed and pending legislation (for example, Goals 2000, the School-to-Work Opportunities Act, and the reauthorization of Title X of the Elementary and Secondary Education Act; see Appendix 2) contain measures to improve the coordination and delivery of social services in the nation's schools. These provisions rightly recognize the need to see that health and social services are available to students who require them, that community services are coordinated with the schools, and that the schools have the flexibility to combine funds from different sources earmarked for coordination.

Improving Research, Data Collection, and Dissemination. The current federal research and dissemination effort is inadequate for an educational system that should emphasize decentralization, flexibility, innovation, and accountability. Such a system requires frequent data collection to monitor the progress of schools and districts in meeting achievement goals. Experimental educational programs need to be rigorously evaluated and the results disseminated so that they can be applied in other schools.

The federal government is the logical sponsor of such research and information dissemination. However, federal capacity to do this is currently insufficient. We recommend expanding federal capacity for educational research and information dissemination. We urge improvements in the quality and frequency of data collection on student achievement, demographic changes, and cost differences among schools, as well as more frequent evaluation and support of innovative educational programs. These data should be collected through consistent research methods so that meaningful comparisons can be made school by school, district by district, and state by state.

# CONCLUSION: PUTTING LEARNING FIRST

A decade of experience with school reform and a wealth of research provide strong evidence on the changes needed in the governance and management of schools to improve student achievement. Both research and experience tell us that the most successful schools focus on learning, have high expectations for academic achievement, reward effort and results, transmit strong positive values, involve parents, and give faculty the authority to make key educational decisions. Creating and sustaining schools that have these characteristics place significant new demands on those directly engaged in the work of education, those in positions of political power who govern and manage the schools, and those in the private sector and the voting public whose support is vital.

The role of governing authorities is clear. They need to set goals, provide resources sufficient to meet those goals, and establish accountability mechanisms that will measure progress and attainment and that will provide information where improvement is needed. Management authority, information, and support must then be transferred to school personnel who are in the best position to determine the curriculum, instructional strategies, and other means to best meet the learning needs of their students. This effort should include parents and other members of the community.

Structural changes will have little effect without major changes in the way students and their parents, teachers, and administrators work, think, and behave. A variety of incentives for both individuals and institutions is needed to motivate these changes in behavior. Among them are clear standards linked to performance-based assessments, as well as rewards and consequences.

No single educational model works for all children. We therefore must be willing to allow schools and districts the latitude to experiment with different approaches and the time to see if they will work.

The lack of hard evidence on specific solutions is not an excuse for inaction. What is needed is bold leadership committed to fundamental change. Given the wide diversity of school systems and student needs, solutions are likely to come in many guises. It is this expected variety that makes a focus on results and decentralized authority so important. Each school must be given the tools it needs to meet its educational challenges and must be held accountable for real progress. The alternative to such bold action is continuation of our current mediocre system.

Free, universal public education has been the cornerstone of the development of the United States as the world's longest-running, large-scale, pluralistic democracy. Now, as ethnic conflicts destroy other societies and our own nation becomes increasingly diverse, it is more important than ever that our public schools function effectively to maintain our democratic way of life.

And they will do that by putting learning first.

# APPENDIX 1

## Enacted Legislation: GOALS 2000
## The National Goals

### TITLE I-NATIONAL EDUCATION GOALS

#### SEC 101 PURPOSE

The purpose of this title is to establish National Education Goals.

#### SEC 102 NATIONAL EDUCATION GOALS

The Congress declares that the National Education Goals are the following

(1) SCHOOL READINESS —

(A) By the year 2000, all children in America will start school ready to learn.

(B) The objectives of this goal are that–

(i) all children will have access to high quality and developmentally appropriate preschool programs that help prepare children for school;

(ii) every parent in the United States will be a child's first teacher and devote time each day to helping such parent's preschool child learn, and parents will have access to the training and support parents need; and

(iii) children will receive the nutrition, physical activity experiences, and health care needed to arrive at school with healthy minds and bodies, and to maintain the mental alertness necessary to be prepared to learn, and the number of low-birthweight babies will be significantly reduced through enhanced prenatal health systems.

(2) SCHOOL COMPLETION —

(A) By the year 2000, the high school graduation rate will increase to at least 90 percent.

(B) The objectives of this goal are that–

(i) the Nation must dramatically reduce its school dropout rate, and 75 percent of the students who do drop out will successfully complete a high school degree or its equivalent; and

(ii) the gap in high school graduation rates between American students from minority backgrounds and their non-minority counterparts will be eliminated.

(3) STUDENT ACHIEVEMENT AND CITIZENSHIP —

(A) By the year 2000, all students will leave grades 4, 8, and 12 having demonstrated competency over challenging subject matter including English, mathematics, science, foreign languages, civics and government, economics, arts, history, and geography, and every school in America will ensure that all students learn to use their minds well, so they may be prepared for responsible citizenship, further learning, and productive employment in our Nation's modern economy.

(B) The objectives for this goal are that–

(i) the academic performance of all students at the elementary and secondary level will increase significantly in every quartile, and the distribution of minority students in each quartile will more closely reflect the student population as a whole;

(ii) the percentage of all students who demonstrate the ability to reason, solve problems, apply knowledge, and write and communicate effectively will increase substantially;

(iii) all students will be involved in activities that promote and demonstrate good citizenship, good health, community service, and personal responsibility;

(iv) all students will have access to physical education and health education to ensure they are healthy and fit;

(v) the percentage of all students who are competent in more than one language will substantially increase; and

(vi) all students will be knowledgeable about the diverse cultural heritage of the Nation and about the world community.

## (4) TEACHER EDUCATION AND PROFESSIONAL DEVELOPMENT —

(A) By the year 2000, the Nation's teaching force will have access to programs for the continued improvement of their professional skills and the opportunity to acquire the knowledge and skills needed to instruct and prepare all American students for the next century.

(B) The objectives for this goal are that–

(i) all teachers will have access to preservice teacher education and continuing professional development activities that will provide such teachers with the knowledge and skills needed to teach to an increasingly diverse student population with a variety of educational, social, and health needs;

(ii) all teachers will have continuing opportunities to acquire additional knowledge and skills needed to teach challenging subject matter and to use emerging new methods, forms of assessment, and technologies;

(iii) States and school districts will create integrated strategies to attract, recruit, prepare, retrain, and support the continued professional development of teachers, administrators, and other educators, so that there is a highly talented work force of professional educa-

tors to teach challenging subject matter; and

(iv) partnerships will be established, whenever possible, among local educational agencies, institutions of higher education, parents, and local labor, business, and professional associations to provide and support programs for the professional development of educators.

## (5) MATHEMATICS AND SCIENCE —

(A) By the year 2000, United States students will be first in the world in mathematics and science achievement.

(B) The objectives of this goal are that–

(i) mathematics and science education, including the metric system of measurement, will be strengthened throughout the system, especially in the early grades;

(ii) the number of teachers with a substantive background in mathematics and science, including the metric system of measurement, will increase by 50 percent; and

(iii) the number of United States undergraduate and graduate students, especially women and minorities, who complete degrees in mathematics, science, and engineering will increase significantly.

## (6) ADULT LITERACY AND LIFELONG LEARNING —

(A) By the year 2000, every adult American will be literate and will possess the knowledge and skills necessary to compete in a global economy and exercise the rights and responsibilities of citizenship.

(B) The objectives for this goal are that–

(i) every major American business will be involved in strengthening the connection between education and work;

(ii) all workers will have the opportunity to acquire the knowledge and skills, from basic to highly technical needed to adapt to emerging new technologies, work methods, and markets through public and private educational, vocational, technical, workplace, or other programs;

(iii) the number of quality programs including those of libraries that are designed to serve more effectively the needs of the growing number of part time and midcareer students will increase substantially;

(iv) the proportion of the qualified students, especially minorities who enter college, who complete at least two years, and who complete their degree programs will increase substantially;

(v) the proportion of college graduates who demonstrate an advanced ability to think critically, communicate effectively, and solve problems will increase substantially; and

(vi) schools, in implementing comprehensive parent involvement programs, will offer more adult literacy, parent training and lifelong learning opportunities to improve the ties between home and school, and enhance parents' work and home lives.

(7) SAFE, DISCIPLINED, AND ALCOHOL- AND DRUG-FREE SCHOOLS —

(A) By the year 2000, every school in the United States will be free of drugs, violence, and the unauthorized presence of firearms and alcohol and will offer a disciplined environment conducive to learning.

(B) The objectives for this goal are that–

(i) every school will implement a firm and fair policy on use, possession, and distribution of drugs and alcohol;

(ii) parents, businesses, governmental and community organizations will work together to ensure the rights of students to study in a safe and secure environment that is free of drugs and crime, and that schools provide a healthy environment and are a safe haven for all children;

(iii) every local educational agency will develop and implement a policy to ensure that all schools are free of violence and the unauthorized presence of weapons;

(iv) every local educational agency will develop a sequential, comprehensive kindergarten through twelfth grade drug and alcohol prevention education program;

(v) drug and alcohol curriculum should be taught as an integral part of sequential, comprehensive health education;

(vi) community based teams should be organized to provide students and teachers with needed support; and

(vii) every school should work to eliminate sexual harassment.

(8) PARENTAL PARTICIPATION —

(A) By the year 2000, every school will promote partnerships that will increase parental involvement and participation in promoting the social, emotional, and academic growth of children.

(B) The objectives for this goal are that–

(i) every State will develop policies to assist local schools and local educational agencies to establish programs for increasing partnerships that respond to the varying needs of parents and the home, including parents of children who are disadvantaged or bilingual, or parents of children with disabilities;

(ii) every school will actively engage parents and families in a partnership which supports the academic work of children at home and shared educational decisionmaking at school; and

(iii) parents and families will help to ensure that schools are adequately supported and will hold schools and teachers to high standards of accountability.

# APPENDIX 2

## Legislative Proposals Regarding Social Services and the Schools

### GOALS 2000

Goals 2000: Educate America legislation was signed into law on March 31, 1994. The law includes Title VII, the "Safe Schools Act of 1994," which authorizes $50 million for school-based safety and violence-prevention services, including the coordination of "school-based activities designed to promote school safety and reduce or prevent school violence and discipline problems with related efforts of education, law enforcement, judicial, health, social service, and other appropriate agencies."

Funds under Title VII will be allocated largely to schools in high-crime areas and are eventually to be integrated with similar efforts initiated by the Drug-Free Schools and Communities Act and the Juvenile Justice and Delinquency Prevention Act of 1974.

### SCHOOL-TO-WORK OPPORTUNITIES ACT

The School-to-Work Opportunities Act passed both houses and was signed into law on May 4, 1994, at the White House. As in Goals 2000, there are no provisions that explicitly call for coordination of social services in the schools. However, there are numerous provisions for coordinating other federal programs with the school-to-work programs.

It is difficult to know just what practical effect these plans and other requirements will have on actual state operation of school-to-work programs. But it would seem that even if some of the above stipulations are followed, the need for coordination of school services will not be lost on participating schools and communities.

### REAUTHORIZATION OF ESEA

On March 24, 1994, the House passed H.R.6, the Elementary and Secondary Education Act Amendments of 1994. This version includes a new Title X that explicitly authorizes the schools to use ESEA funds to hire a full-time coordinator of social services. Jack Jennings, Counsel to the Subcommittee on Elementary, Secondary and Vocational Education, recently attributed the inclusion of this title to testimony given by James J. Renier in January 1992 on behalf of CED.

More specifically, Title X authorizes the creation of "coordinated services projects" to meet the educational, health, social service, and other needs of children and their families and their foster families through a community-wide partnership that links public and private agencies, providing such services or access to such services through a coordination site at or near a school.

Funds are allowed to be used for a number of coordinating activities, including hiring a services coordinator, making minor renovations to existing buildings for the delivery of services, and improving coordination and information sharing between members of the coordinated services partnership.

## THE HEALTH SECURITY ACT

Subtitle G of Title III of President Clinton's Health Security Act calls for spending over $2 billion on comprehensive school health education and school-related health service programs.

There are two main features: an education effort to be run by states and local schools (K-12) targeted at health-risk behaviors among students, including tobacco, alcohol and other drug use; sexual behavior; HIV; dietary behavior; and a multibillion-dollar effort through states and local community partnerships to develop school health service sites.

Funds under these provisions are designed to provide health services to K-12 students not covered by any other insurer and will be targeted to at-risk communities with high levels of poverty, large numbers of medically unserved, and high rates of health risk among schoolchildren, including HIV, adolescent pregnancy, drug abuse, community and gang violence.

Both the education and the services components call for considerable integration with existing social service and health service programs.

# NOTES

## CHAPTER 1

1. Several of the major themes of this statement, in particular the importance of setting performance standards, providing appropriate incentives, and organizing resources efficiently, are emphasized and extensively documented in Eric A. Hanushek with others, *Making Schools Work: Improving Performance and Controlling Costs* (Washington, D.C.: The Brookings Institution, in press).

2. *Investing in Our Children: Business and the Public Schools* (1985), p. 20; *Children in Need: Investment Strategies for the Educationally Disadvantaged* (1987), p. 43.

3. *Investing in Our Children: Business and the Public Schools, Children in Need: Investment Strategies for the Educationally Disadvantaged, The Unfinished Agenda: A New Vision for Education and Child Development* (1991).

4. *An Assessment of American Education: The View of Employers, Higher Educators, The Public, Recent Students, and Their Parents* (1991).

5. The National Commission on Time and Learning, *Prisoners of Time* (Washington, D.C.: U.S. Government Printing Office, 1994), p. 25.

## CHAPTER 2

1. Anthony P. Carnevale and Jeffrey D. Porro, *Quality Education: School Reform for the New American Economy* (Washington, D.C.: U.S. Department of Education, Office of Educational Research and Improvement, 1994), p. 12.

2. U.S. Department of Education, National Center for Education Statistics, *The Condition of Education, 1993* (Washington, D.C.: U.S. Government Printing Office, 1993), pp. 40-47.

3. U.S. Department of Education, National Center for Education Statistics, *Trends in Academic Progress* (Washington, D.C.: U.S. Government Printing Office, 1991), pp. 4-8.

4. See, for example, U.S. Department of Education, National Center for Education Statistics, *International Mathematics and Science Assessments: What Have We Learned?* (Washington, D.C.: U.S. Government Printing Office, 1992); or Organization for Economic Cooperation and Development, Centre for Educational Research and Innovation, *Education at a Glance: OECD Indicators* (Paris: OECD, 1993), pp. 160-171.

5. Organization for Economic Cooperation and Development, *Education at a Glance: OECD Indicators*, p. 155.

6. Educational Testing Service, Policy Information Center, *Education Issues of the 1990s* (Princeton, N.J.: Educational Testing Service, 1993).

7. "Becoming American, Habits and All," *New York Times*, February 23, 1994, p. B 7:4.

8. John Chubb and Terry Moe, *Politics, Markets, and America's Schools* (Washington, D.C.: The Brookings Institution, 1990), p. 140; Anthony Bryk, Valerie Lee, and Julia Smith, "High School Organization and Its Effects on Teachers and Students," in *Choice and Control in American Education*, vol. 1, ed. William H. Clune and John F. Witte (London: The Falmer Press, 1990), pp. 176-177; Paul Hill and Tamar Gendler, *High Schools of Character* (Santa Monica, Calif.: The RAND Corporation, 1991); and Charles Teddlie and Sam Stringfield, *Schools Make a Difference: Lessons Learned from a 10-Year Study of School Effects* (New York: Teachers College Press, Teachers College, Columbia University, 1993).

9. See Hill and Gendler, *High Schools of Character*; Bryk, Lee, and Smith, "High School Organization and Its Effects on Teachers and Students"; and Teddlie and Stringfield, *Schools Make a Difference: Lessons Learned from a 10-Year Study of School Effects*.

10. Hill and Gendler, *High Schools of Character*.

11. Hill and Gendler, *High Schools of Character*.

12. Bruce Bimber, *School Decentralization: Lessons from the Study of Bureaucracy* (Santa Monica, Calif.: The RAND Corporation, 1993), pp. 29-31.

13. Hill and Gendler, *High Schools of Character*.

14. Paul T. Hill and Josephine Bonan, *Decentralization and Accountability in Public Education* (Santa Monica, Calif.: The RAND Corporation, 1991), p. 12.

15. Hill and Bonan, *Decentralization and Accountability in Public Education*, p. 11.

16. *Closer Look*, no. 4 (Chicago, Ill.: Designs for Change, January 1994).

17. Anita A. Summers and Amy W. Johnson, "A Review of the Evidence on the Effects of School-Based Management Plans" (Panel on the Economics of Educational Reform and Teaching, Washington, D.C., May 29, 1991), pp. 2, 10-12; *Site-Based Management*, Information Folio (Arlington, Va.: Educational Research Service, 1990).

18. Nancy A. Madden, Robert E. Slavin, Nancy L. Karweit, Lawrence J. Dolan, and Barbara A. Wasik, "Success for All: Longitudinal Effects of a Restructuring Program for Inner-City Elementary Schools," *American Educational Research Journal* 30, no. 1 (Spring 1993): 123-148.

19. Jane McCarthy and Suzanne Still, "Hollibrook Accelerated Elementary School," in *Restructuring Schooling*, ed. Joseph Murphy and Paul Mallinger (Monterrey Park, Calif.: Corwin Press, 1993), pp. 63-83.

20. Priscilla Wohlstetter and Roxane Smeyer, "New Boundaries for School-Based Management: The High Involvement Model" (paper presented at the Fifteenth Annual Research Conference of the Association for Public Policy Analysis and Management, Washington, D.C., October 28-30), 1993.

21. Wohlstetter and Smeyer, "New Boundaries for School-Based Management: The High School Involvement Model."

22. Hill and Bonan, *Decentralization and Accountability in Public Education*, pp. 10-11.

23. Wohlstetter and Smeyer, "New Boundaries for School-Based Management: The High School Involvement Model."

24. Carnevale and Porro, *Quality Education: School Reform for the New American Economy*, p. 60.

25. Charles Kerchner Taylor and Julia E. Koppich, *A Union of Professionals: Labor Relations and Educational Reform* (New York: Teachers College Press, Teachers College, Columbia University, 1993), p. 1.

26. Mary Jordan, "Charter Schools Rewrite Public Lesson Plan," *Washington Post*, April 30, 1994.

27. The Carnegie Foundation for the Advancement of Teaching, *School Choice* (Princeton, N.J.: Carnegie Foundation for the Advancement of Teaching, 1992), p. 15.

28. Joseph Nathan, *Facts, Figures, and Faces: A Look At Minnesota's School Choice Programs* (Minneapolis, Minn.: University of Minnesota, Center for School Change, November 1993).

29. Joseph Nathan, ed., *Public Schools by Choice* (Minneapolis, Minn.: Free Spirit Press, 1989).

30. Children Now, *What School Choice Means for Children* (Oakland, Calif.: Children Now, September 1993).

31. John F. Witte, *Third Year Report: Milwaukee Parental Choice Program* (Madison, Wisc.: University of Wisconsin–Madison, Department of Political Science and The Robert M. La Follette Institute of Public Affairs, December 1993).

32. National Institute of Justice, Washington, D.C., personal correspondence.

33. Bimber, *School Decentralization: Lessons from the Study of Bureaucracy*, pp. 18-19.

34. Albert Shanker, "A Proposal for Using Incentives for Restructuring Our Public Schools," *Aspen Institute Quarterly* 3, no. 2 (Spring 1991): 72-108.

35. Jason N. Juffras and Isabel V. Sawhill, "Putting Excellence Back Into Education," *Policy Bites*, vol. 10 (Washington, D.C.: The Urban Institute, January 1992), p. 2.

36. Susan Johnson, "Incentives for Teachers: What Motivates, What Matters," *Educational Administration Quarterly* 22 (Summer 1986): 73.

37. Ann Weaver Hart and Michael J. Murphy, "New Teachers React to Redesigned Teacher Work," *American Journal of Education* (May 1990): 244.

38. J. Edward Kellogh and Haoran Lu, "The Paradox of Merit Pay in the Public Sector: Persistence of a Problematic Procedure," *Review of Public Personnel Administration* (Spring 1993): 64.

39. See The Conference Board, *Variable Pay: Nontraditional Programs for Motivation and Reward* (New York: The Conference Board, 1993), a survey of pay-for-performance practices of 382 companies; and George Milkovich and Carolyn Milkovich, "Strengthening the Pay-Performance Relationship: The Research," *Compensation & Benefits Review* (November-December 1992): 53-62.

40. Richard J. Murnane and David K. Cohen, "Merit Pay and the Evaluation Problem: Why Most Merit Pay Plans Fail and a Few Survive," *Harvard Educational Review* 56 (February 1986): 1-17.

41. Edwin M. Bridges, *The Incompetent Teacher: The Challenge and the Response* (Philadelphia: The Falmer Press, 1986), p. 89-90.

42. Kerchner and Koppich, *A Union of Professionals: Labor Relations and Educational Reform*, pp. 20-24.

43. Kerchner and Koppich, *A Union of Professionals: Labor Relations and Educational Reform*, pp. 22.

44. Kerchner and Koppich, *A Union of Professionals: Labor Relations and Educational Reform*, pp. 20-21.

45. John Bishop, *The Economic Consequences of Schooling and Learning* (Washington, D.C.: Economic Policy Institute, 1984), p. 45-48.

46. John Bishop, *The Economic Consequences of Schooling and Learning*, pp. 45-48.

47. Margaret Brown, "Problematic Issues in National Assessment," *Cambridge Journal of Education* 21, no. 2 (1991): 215-229.

48. Kenneth A. Couch, "Germans and Job Training, Education, and Us," *American Enterprise* (November-December 1993): 16.

49. Edward Pauly, Hilary Kopp, and Joshua Haimson, *Home-Grown Lessons: Innovative Programs Linking Work and High School* (New York: Manpower Demonstration Research Corporation, January 1994), Table 1.1.

50. Paul Osterman and Maria Iannozzi, *Youth Apprenticeships and School-to-Work Transition: Current Knowledge and Legislative Strategy*, Working Paper no. 14 (Washington, D.C.: National Center on the Educational Quality of the Workforce, 1993), pp. 19-20.

51. "School-to-Work Bill Heads to President," *Congressional Quarterly* 52, no. 16 (April 23, 1994): 1009.

## CHAPTER 3

1. *Facing the Challenge: The Report of The Twentieth Century Fund Task Force on School Governance* (New York: The Twentieth Century Fund Press, 1992), pp. 47-48.

2. Jacqueline P. Danzberger, "School Boards: A Troubled American Institution," (background paper prepared for The Twentieth Century Fund–Danforth Foundation Task Force on School Governance, May 1991), p. ii.

3. Danzberger, "School Boards: A Troubled American Institution," p. ii.

4. Danzberger, "School Boards: A Troubled American Institution," p. 31.

5. Jacqueline P. Danzberger, Michael W. Kirst, Michael D. Usdan, *Governing Public Schools: New Times, New Requirements* (Washington, D.C.: Institute for Educational Leadership, 1992), p. 30.

6. Michael Fix and Daphne Kenyon, eds., *Coping With Mandates: What Are the Alternatives?* (Washington, D.C.: Urban Institute Press, 1990), p. 7.

7. The Educational Research Service, *The Urban Superintendent Turnover* (Arlington, Va.: The Educational Research Service, 1992).

8. Danzberger, Kirst, and Usdan, *Governing Public Schools: New Times, New Requirements*, pp. 52-53.

9. *Facing the Challenge: The Report of the Twentieth Century Fund Task Force on School Governance*, p. 5.

10. *Facing the Challenge: The Report of the Twentieth Century Fund Task Force on School Governance*, pp. 58-59.

11. Davis W. Campbell and Diane Greene, "Defining the Leadership Role of School Boards in the 21st Century," *Phi Delta Kappan* (January 1994): 391-395.

12. Danzberger, Kirst, Usdan, *Governing Public Schools: New Times, New Requirements*, p. 60.

13. Danzberger, Kirst, Usdan, *Governing Public Schools: New Times, New Requirements*, pp. 59-60.

14. *Facing the Challenge: The Report of the Twentieth Century Fund Task Force on School Governance*, pp. 9-11.

15. *New Mexico's Children's Agenda* (1993), p. 6.

16. Educational Testing Service, Policy Information Center, *The State of Inequality* (Princeton, N.J.: Educational Testing Service, 1991), 28.

17. Allen Odden, "Including School Finance in Systemic Reform Strategies: A Commentary," *CPRE Finance Briefs* (New Brunswick, N.J.: Consortium for Policy Research in Education, May 1994), p. 4.

18. E. A. Hanushek, "The Impact of Differential Expenditures on School Performance," *Educational Researcher* 18, no. 4 (1989): 45-46, and others found that available studies revealed "no strong or systematic relationship between school expenditures and student performance." A recent meta-analysis of the same research by L. V. Hedges, R. D. Laine, and R. Greenwald concluded that "money does matter somewhere" (see "Does Money Matter? A Meta-Analysis of Studies of the Effects of Differential School Inputs on Student Outcomes," *Educational Researcher* 23, no. 3 (April 1994). Both conclusions are consistent with our view.

19. Stephen M. Barro, "What Does the Education Dollar Buy?: Relationships of Staffing, Staff Characteristics, and Staff Salaries to State Per-Pupil Spending," CPRE Finance Center: Integrated Multilevel Resource-Use Study, State-Level Analysis — Part I, November 1992.

20. Mary Levy, Washington Lawyers Commission, personal communication.

21. Catholic Archdiocese of Washington, Office of the Superintendent, personal communication.

22. The Partnership for New Jersey, *"Doing It Better": Good Education at Lower Costs*, School District Efficiency Study, January 1994; interviews with Dr. James Caulfield, district superintendent.

23. Janet Froetscher, executive director, Financial Research and Advisory Committee, personal communication.

24. William Clune, "The Shift from Equity to Adequacy in School Finance" (research paper supported by the Center for Policy Research in Education and the Wisconsin Center for Education Research, University of Wisconsin–Madison, (June 1993), pp. 5-6.

25. Joseph E. Stiglitz, *Economics of the Public Sector* (New York: W. W. Norton, 1986), p. 377.

# MEMORANDA OF COMMENT, RESERVATION, OR DISSENT

## Page 7, ARNOLD R. WEBER

This is an excellent statement, particularly the early and consistent emphasis on returning the schools to their central mission—education—rather than serving as an all-purpose social ameliorative.

## Page 9, PRES KABACOFF

I believe this is an excellent report, one that has the potential to drive the debate on education reform in new directions. I would, however, like to emphasize the importance of bringing students into the process of remaking our schools.

As the report points out, students need to feel they are a part of a community of learning. I believe this can be advanced significantly through concerted efforts to develop peer-assistance programs which would produce a more positive and productive school experience for all students.

An excellent example of such a program is PAL (Peer Assistance and Leadership) Program which began as a pilot effort at one Austin, Texas high school in 1980 and by 1987 had grown so successful that it inspired the launching of a statewide project entitled the Peer Assistance Network of Texas, or PAN–Texas, which has been instrumental in the replication and support of the program in over 400 school districts throughout the state.

PAL makes sense for three reasons: (1) There are more needs in the schools than can be met by adult professional staff. (2) Properly selected, trained, and supervised, students themselves can be effective in meeting many of those needs. (3) As students assist other students, the "labor" is free, and the benefits are bi-directional.

Among the many peer-assistance services provided by PAL students:

- peer support, positive role models, and a "listening ear" to other students, on both an individual and group basis

- school orientation of new/transferred students, including assistance with the transition from elementary to middle, or middle to high school

- peer tutoring and other services aimed at promoting academic achievement

- structured presentations on such topics as school adjustment, substance-abuse prevention, peer relations, violence prevention, multicultural issues, and other issues of interest or concern to young people

- assistance to students with special needs

- specialized services in such areas as peer mediation, group facilitation, community service learning and outreach projects

Page 18, JAMES Q. RIORDAN

I believe that we are too negative and restrictive about choice. Meaningful choice for children to attend private schools that are free from overregulation (and special public schools that have been liberated from excessive political and bureaucratic mandates) should be encouraged. Many (but of course not all) of the choice schools will succeed and draw students. That competition will help legislators, school boards, administrators, and unions to focus on the need to put in place the needed reforms for mainline public schools.

Page 24, PETER A. BENOLIEL, with which FRANKLIN A. LINDSAY has asked to be associated.

This is the most critical recommendation in this statement. Unless the individual student (and, in turn, his/her parents) takes personal responsibility for the learning process, nothing will happen, the other recommendations notwithstanding. Clear linkages must be established between student performance and opportunities for higher education, financial assistance, and employment. This recommendation is the sine qua non of this statement.

# FUNDERS

We wish to give special thanks to the following foundations and companies whose generous support made this policy statement possible:

Aetna Foundation, Inc.
American Express Foundation
ARCO Chemical Company
Bell Atlantic
Carnegie Corporation of New York
Exxon Education Foundation
GTE Foundation
The George Gund Foundation
Honeywell Foundation
International Paper Company Foundation
Lilly Endowment, Inc.
Metropolitan Life Foundation
Mobil Foundation, Inc.
Morgan Stanley Group Inc.
Charles Stewart Mott Foundation
The Pew Charitable Trusts
The Prudential Foundation

# OBJECTIVES OF THE COMMITTEE FOR ECONOMIC DEVELOPMENT

For more than 50 years, the Committee for Economic Development has been a respected influence on the formation of business and public policy. CED is devoted to these two objectives:

*To develop, through objective research and informed discussion, findings and recommendations for private and public policy that will contribute to preserving and strengthening our free society, achieving steady economic growth at high employment and reasonably stable prices, increasing productivity and living standards, providing greater and more equal opportunity for every citizen, and improving the quality of life for all.*

*To bring about increasing understanding by present and future leaders in business, government, and education, and among concerned citizens, of the importance of these objectives and the ways in which they can be achieved.*

CED's work is supported by private voluntary contributions from business and industry, foundations, and individuals. It is independent, nonprofit, nonpartisan, and nonpolitical.

Through this business-academic partnership, CED endeavors to develop policy statements and other research materials that commend themselves as guides to public and business policy; that can be used as texts in college economics and political science courses and in management training courses; that will be considered and discussed by newspaper and magazine editors, columnists, and commentators; and that are distributed abroad to promote better understanding of the American economic system.

CED believes that by enabling business leaders to demonstrate constructively their concern for the general welfare, it is helping business to earn and maintain the national and community respect essential to the successful functioning of the free enterprise capitalist system.

# CED HONORARY TRUSTEES

# STATEMENTS ON NATIONAL POLICY ISSUED BY THE COMMITTEE FOR ECONOMIC DEVELOPMENT

## SELECTED PUBLICATIONS:

Prescription for Progress: The Uruguay Round in the New Global Economy *(1994)*

*From Promise to Progress: Towards a New Stage in U.S.-Japan Economic Relations *(1994)*

U.S. Trade Policy Beyond The Uruguay Round *(1994)*

In Our Best Interest: NAFTA and the New American Economy *(1993)*

What Price Clean Air? A Market Approach to Energy and Environmental Policy *(1993)*

Why Child Care Matters? Preparing Young Children For A More Productive America *(1993)*

Restoring Prosperity: Budget Choices for Economic Growth *(1992)*

The United States in the New Global Economy: A Rallier of Nations *(1992)*

The Economy and National Defense: Adjusting to Cutbacks in the Post-Cold War Era *(1991)*

Politics, Tax Cuts and the Peace Dividend *(1991)*

The Unfinished Agenda: A New Vision for Child Development and Education *(1991)*

Foreign Investment in the United States: What Does It Signal? *(1990)*

An America That Works: The Life-Cycle Approach to a Competitive Work Force *(1990)*

Breaking New Ground in U.S. Trade Policy *(1990)*

Battling America's Budget Deficits *(1989)*

*Strengthening U.S.-Japan Economic Relations *(1989)*

Who Should Be Liable? A Guide to Policy for Dealing with Risk *(1989)*

Investing in America's Future: Challenges and Opportunities for Public Sector Economic Policies *(1988)*

Children in Need: Investment Strategies for the Educationally Disadvantaged *(1987)*

Finance and Third World Economic Growth *(1987)*

Toll of the Twin Deficits *(1987)*

Reforming Health Care: A Market Prescription *(1987)*

Work and Change: Labor Market Adjustment Policies in a Competitive World *(1987)*

Leadership for Dynamic State Economies *(1986)*

Investing in Our Children: Business and the Public Schools *(1985)*

Fighting Federal Deficits: The Time for Hard Choices *(1985)*

Strategy for U.S. Industrial Competitiveness *(1984)*

Strengthening the Federal Budget Process: A Requirement for Effective Fiscal Control *(1983)*

Productivity Policy: Key to the Nation's Economic Future *(1983)*

Energy Prices and Public Policy *(1982)*

Public-Private Partnership: An Opportunity for Urban Communities *(1982)*

Reforming Retirement Policies *(1981)*

Transnational Corporations and Developing Countries: New Policies for a Changing World Economy *(1981)*

Fighting Inflation and Rebuilding a Sound Economy *(1980)*

Stimulating Technological Progress *(1980)*

*Statements issued in association with CED counterpart organizations in foreign countries.

# CED COUNTERPART ORGANIZATIONS

Close relations exist between the Committee for Economic Development and independent, nonpolitical research organizations in other countries. Such counterpart groups are composed of business executives and scholars and have objectives similar to those of CED, which they pursue by similarly objective methods. CED cooperates with these organizations on research and study projects of common interest to the various countries concerned. This program has resulted in a number of joint policy statements involving such international matters as energy, East-West trade, assistance to developing countries, and the reduction of nontariff barriers to trade.

| | |
|---|---|
| **CE** | Circulo de Empresarios<br>Madrid, Spain |
| **CEDA** | Committee for Economic Development of Australia<br>Sydney, Australia |
| **CEPES** | Vereinigung für Wirtschaftlichen Fortschritt E.V.<br>Frankfurt, Germany |
| **FAE** | Forum de Administradores de Empresas<br>Lisbon, Portugal |
| **IE** | Institut de l'Entreprise<br>Brussels, Belgium |
| **IE** | Institut de l'Entreprise<br>Paris, France |
| **IDW** | Institut der Deutschen Wirtschaft<br>Cologne, Germany |
| **経済同友会** | Keizai Doyukai<br>Tokyo, Japan |
| **SMO** | Stichting Maatschappij en Onderneming,<br>The Netherlands |
| **SNS** | Studieförbundet Naringsliv och Samhälle<br>Stockholm, Sweden |